ENDORSEMENTS

Tim Bonnell Jr. has created a breakthrough success system by embracing how his brain works. Quit Jacking Around is full of clear, doable frameworks—especially GAIN and JACKED—that make it so much easier to take action and follow through. It's an energizing read that helps you win your own game.

—Shannon Waller
Author of the *Team Success Handbook* and *Multiplication by Subtraction*

Quit Jacking Around cuts straight to the core of what truly moves a life forward: clarity, structure, and consistent action. This book isn't about hype; it's about building a personal success system anchored in who you are and who you're becoming. What I love is how it empowers you to align your vision, habits, and identity so progress becomes inevitable. If you're ready to stop negotiating with your potential and start creating the future you can feel inside you, this book hands you the framework to make it real, repeatable, and yours.

—Chad T. Jenkins
SEEDSPARK

As someone who equips leaders to scale with purpose, I recognize the power of a clear, repeatable success system—and Tim delivers exactly that. *Quit Jacking Around* offers the mindset, structure, and accountability every leader needs but rarely builds on their own. This is more than a motivational read; it's a guidebook for meaningful, sustained personal transformation.

If you're ready to create change that lasts, this book will show you the way.

—Ethan Martin
PFD Group, Inc.

Tim gets to the heart of why so many goals fail—lack of a system. *Quit Jacking Around* gives you a practical roadmap for building the mindset, structure, and accountability needed to turn vision into results.

—Mike Torrey
Torrey Advisory Group

If you've got goals, this book is for you. In *Quit Jacking Around*, Tim uses his own life, challenges, and triumphs to create a roadmap we can all follow. He goes straight to the biggest barrier we face, uncovering what truly motivates us, and offers a clear, practical system to act on it. Read it, follow and make big things happen.

—Mary Fearon
OnPrpose

QUIT JACKING AROUND

BUILD YOUR WINNING PERSONAL SUCCESS SYSTEM™

UNLOCK YOUR POTENTIAL WITH A PROVEN SYSTEM FOR SETTING, TRACKING, AND ACHIEVING YOUR GOALS

More Books from CoVerse Collective

Seedspark.com/CoVerse

QUIT JACKING AROUND

BUILD YOUR WINNING PERSONAL SUCCESS SYSTEM™

UNLOCK YOUR POTENTIAL WITH A PROVEN SYSTEM FOR SETTING, TRACKING, AND ACHIEVING YOUR GOALS

Timothy K. Bonnell Jr.

CoVerse COLLECTIVE

QUIT JACKING AROUND © 2026 by Timothy K. Bonnell Jr.

Printed in the United States of America

Published by Igniting Souls
PO Box 43, Powell, OH 43065
IgnitingSouls.com

This book contains material protected under international and federal copyright laws and treaties. Any unauthorized reprint or use of this material is prohibited. No part of this book may be reproduced or transmitted in any form or by any means, electronic or mechanical, including photocopying, recording, or by any information storage and retrieval system, without express written permission from the author.

LCCN: 2025915842
Paperback ISBN: 978-1-63680-549-8
Hardcover ISBN: 978-1-63680-550-4
e-Book ISBN: 978-1-63680-551-1

Available in paperback, hardcover, e-book, and audiobook.

All Scripture quotations, unless otherwise indicated, are taken from the Holy Bible, New International Version®, NIV®. Copyright © 1973, 1978, 1984 by Biblica, Inc.™ Used by permission of Zondervan. All rights reserved worldwide.

Any Internet addresses (websites, blogs, etc.) and telephone numbers printed in this book are offered as a resource. They are not intended in any way to be or imply an endorsement by Igniting Souls, nor does Igniting Souls vouch for the content of these sites and numbers for the life of this book.

Some names and identifying details may have been changed
to protect the privacy of individuals.

The content of this book reflects the author's personal experiences, opinions, and interpretations. The inclusion of any individual, living or deceased, or any organization or entity, is not intended to malign, defame, or harm the reputation of such persons or entities. All statements regarding individuals are solely the author's perspective and do not represent verified facts unless expressly cited to a verifiable source.

The publisher has not independently investigated or confirmed the accuracy of any such references and disclaims all responsibility for them. Nothing in this book should be construed as factual assertions about the character, conduct, or reputation of any individual or entity mentioned. Any resemblance to persons living or dead is purely coincidental unless explicitly stated.

The publisher expressly disclaims liability for any alleged loss, damage, or injury arising from any perceived defamatory content or reliance upon statements within this work. Responsibility for the views, depictions, and representations rests solely with the author.

DISCLAIMERS

The contents of *Quit Jacking Around* and its related materials—whether presented in print, digital, audio, or live formats—are provided for educational, informational, and self-development purposes only. No part of this publication is intended to offer or substitute for medical, psychological, financial, legal, or other professional advice.

While this book and its associated tools are designed to support growth, clarity, and goal achievement, results will vary depending on individual circumstances, background, motivation, and application. The strategies and methods described herein are offered in good faith, based on the author's personal experience and professional insights, but no guarantees are made regarding specific outcomes or success.

Any participation in coaching, training, or certification programs associated with the Personal Success System™ is voluntary and undertaken at the participant's own risk. By engaging with this content or related programs, you agree that the author, publisher, affiliates, certified coaches, or licensees shall not be held liable for any damages, direct or indirect, that may arise from the use or misuse of the information provided.

Certification and licensing programs, where applicable, do not confer professional or legal credentials, nor do they imply endorsement beyond the scope explicitly defined in the program materials. Individuals seeking to provide coaching or advisory services are solely responsible for adhering to any legal, regulatory, or professional standards required in their jurisdiction.

All trademarks, program names, and system components are the intellectual property of the author and may not be copied, reproduced, or used without prior written consent, except as permitted by law or explicit license agreement.

TABLE OF CONTENTS

Introduction: The Missing Link to Your Success. xiii

PART 1: MINDSET

Chapter 1: Preparing Your Mind for Growth 5
Chapter 2: Establishing a Winning Mindset. 12
Chapter 3: Cognitive Biases 31
Chapter 4: Transformational Thinking. 38
Chapter 5: Winning the War of the Mind 49
Practical Application in Building Your Personal Success
    System: Mindset. 66
Section Summary and Key Takeaways: Mindset 67

PART 2: DNA

Chapter 6: Discovering Your DNA. 73
Chapter 7: Defining Your Purpose with GRIT 84
Chapter 8: Discover Your DNA—Step 2:
    Gain Clarity on Your Personal Values 96
The Power of Understanding Your DNA
    (Purpose + Values) in Achieving Your Goals 103
Discovering Your DNA Summary 104

PART 3: VISION

Chapter 9: Crafting Your Vision for the Future 109
Section Summary: Vision 129

PART 4: GOALS

Chapter 10: Goals: The Bridge Between Vision and
    Reality 135
Chapter 11: Establishing Habits and Actions:
    Turning Vision Into Reality One Day at a Time 157
Chapter 12: Tracking Habits as Key Performance
    Indicators (KPIs) 174
Section Summary: Goal Setting in the Quit Jacking
    Around Personal Success System 192

PART 5: EXECUTION

Chapter 13: Execution: Sustaining Momentum and
    Staying Accountable 205
Chapter 14: Execution Strategies and Tools:
    Make Habits Automatic and Unstoppable 231
Chapter 15: Accountability and Support: Success Is a
    Team Effort 254
Section Summary: Execution: Sustaining Momentum
    and Staying Accountable 268
Conclusion 273
Quit Jacking Around
    Personal Success System Commitment 277
Endnotes 279
Acknowledgments 291
About the Author 293

INTRODUCTION: THE MISSING LINK TO YOUR SUCCESS

Have you ever felt the gap between your aspirations and your accomplishments? Have you ever set lofty goals only to find yourself falling short, discouraged, or simply overwhelmed by the enormity of the task?

You're not alone.

Most people don't fail because they lack ambition; they fail because they lack the systems to bridge the gap between their dreams and reality. As James Clear wrote in *Atomic Habits*, "You do not rise to the level of your goals. You fall to the level of your systems."[1]

THE RESOLUTION ILLUSION: WHY GOOD INTENTIONS FAIL WITHOUT A SYSTEM

Every January, millions of people step into the new year with high hopes and bold declarations. It's a cultural ritual, the tradition of New Year's resolutions. People resolve to get fit, read more, spend less, or finally launch that dream project. There's energy in the air, an intoxicating mix of optimism and momentum. Change feels inevitable.

Yet, within a few short weeks, that optimism crashes headfirst into reality as the Resolution Illusion™ sets in.

Between 38.5 percent and 41 percent of US adults set New Year's resolutions each year, with 59 percent of young adults (ages eighteen to thirty-four) being the most likely to participate.[2] [3] At the start, an overwhelming 87 percent of people report feeling confident that they'll succeed.[4] But what actually happens?

By February, **80 percent** of those resolutions have already failed.[5]

The drop-off is swift.

- **23 percent** give up within the first week.[6] [7]
- **64 percent** abandon their resolutions after just one month.[8]
- **"Quitter's Day,"** the second Friday of January, marks a sharp decline in commitment.[9]
- By the end of January, **43 percent** throw in the towel.[10]

In the end, only 9 percent of Americans stick with their resolutions for the entire year.[11] [12]

THE GAP BETWEEN HOPE AND HABIT

Why do so many fail?

According to surveys, these are some of the top reasons:[13]

- **35 percent** say they *lose motivation*.
- **19 percent** feel *too busy* to follow through.

- **18 percent** end up *changing their goals or priorities* altogether.

The message is clear: People aren't failing because they lack discipline; they're failing because they lack a *system*.

Quit Jacking Around™ is built to address that gap. It isn't about motivation, gimmicks, or fleeting inspiration. It's about structure, creating a repeatable, sustainable framework that moves you from intention to transformation.

BEYOND RESOLUTIONS: HOW PEOPLE APPROACH GOALS

This pattern isn't limited to January. In fact, the broader data on goal-setting are just as sobering.[14]

- Only 20 percent of people set personal goals at all.
- Of those, only 30 percent achieve them.
- Fewer than 3 percent of Americans actually *write down* their goals.
- The research offers powerful insight. Writing down your goals dramatically improves your odds of success. People who write down their goals are 42 percent more likely to achieve them. That number increases as more structure is added.
- 61 percent of written goals are achieved, compared to 43 percent of unwritten ones.
- Add an action plan and share it with a friend? Your success rate jumps to 64 percent.
- Report weekly progress to an accountability partner? You're looking at a 76 percent success rate.

These numbers aren't just interesting; they're instructive. They tell us that the key to meaningful change isn't more willpower; it's *clarity* and *accountability*. A goal without a system is a wish. Wishes are no match for stress, distraction, and decision fatigue.

Quit Jacking Around starts with mindset and purpose, then equips you with tools to build a Personal Success System™ (PSS) that's grounded in your values, vision, and daily habits. With the right framework, you'll stop relying on calendar-based motivation and start becoming the person who makes things happen all year long. It's not magic; it's a method.

MY STORY

Just a few years ago, I was nearly ninety pounds heavier than I am today. In March 2020, coinciding with the onset of the COVID-19 pandemic, I reached a breaking point. I knew I needed to make a change. I needed to lose weight and improve my health.

Like many others, I had tried various methods, including eating better, exercising, and experimenting with different approaches, but nothing seemed to create lasting results. What I eventually realized was that the key to success wasn't just about diet or exercise; it started with my *mindset*.

I had to replace the limiting beliefs that held me back for years, thoughts like *I can't lose weight* or *nothing ever works*, with empowering truths. I reminded myself that I *was* capable, that discipline was within reach, and that if I had a clear purpose, the right strategies, and the right support system, I *could* achieve my goal.

With this mental shift, everything changed. Over the next six to twelve months, I stayed committed to the process, and the weight began to come off. More importantly, my mindset continued to evolve, reinforcing new habits and a healthier lifestyle.

The lesson was clear: Lasting change begins in the mind. You can't keep doing the same things and expecting different results. True transformation starts with shifting your beliefs, redefining what is possible, and committing to the process.

After addressing my mindset, the next crucial step in my weight loss journey was gaining clarity on my *purpose* and *values (DNA)*, the *why* behind my decision to lose weight and improve my health.

Many people want to lose weight simply to feel better. While that was certainly part of my motivation, my reasons ran deeper. As a father of four children, two of whom have special needs and are under the age of ten, I knew that my health directly impacted my ability to care for them. My family relied on me, as did my employees and my business. I needed the energy, strength, and longevity to continue serving those who depended on me.

Beyond those responsibilities, I was also tired of feeling sluggish, drained, and physically weak. I wanted to regain the energy to be present with my family, to feel strong and capable, and to enjoy the benefits of better health. The reward for my effort would be more time with my loved ones, greater vitality, and a renewed sense of confidence.

Understanding my *why* gave me powerful motivation. I didn't just think about it; I wrote it down. I documented my reasons and structured them into a plan that would keep me focused. Every time I faced challenges, I reminded myself why I started.

With the right mindset in place and a clear purpose driving me forward, I was ready for the next step. I had to develop a *vision* of my future health that I could turn into reality.

I needed to go beyond the general goal of "losing weight" and define exactly what *being healthy* would look like for me. That meant sitting down and identifying specific targets: How much weight did I need to lose? What should my body mass index (BMI) be? What key health markers, such as blood pressure, cholesterol, and other biomarkers, did I need to improve?

Weight loss is just one indicator of health. My goal was more than shedding pounds; I wanted true, sustainable well-being.

To ensure I was setting the right targets, I consulted with my doctor and a nutritionist, gathering expert insights on what a healthy version of *me* should look like. With their guidance, I mapped out my ideal weight, body composition, and overall health metrics.

My vision wasn't just about numbers. I took time to visualize how I would *feel* once I reached my goal, how much more energy I'd have, how differently my body would move, and what size clothing I would wear. The clearer I became about my desired outcome, the more motivated I was to take action.

After establishing the right mindset, clarifying my purpose and values, and developing a clear vision for my health, the next step was to put that vision into action. Defining my goals was one thing; executing them required a structured, measurable plan.

To ensure progress, I broke the long-term goal of losing ninety pounds into smaller, achievable milestones. Instead of focusing solely on the final number, I created quarterly targets, allowing me to celebrate short-term wins along the way. This approach helped maintain momentum and provided a clear roadmap toward success.

I applied my own version of the SMART goal framework, ensuring my goals were Specific, Measurable, Attainable, Relevant, and Time-bound. More on my framework will come later in the book. This meant:

- Following a specific nutrition plan tailored to my health needs
- Implementing a structured exercise regimen
- Tracking my weight and body composition daily
- Scheduling quarterly blood tests to monitor biomarkers and overall health progress

I also set up a system for consistently measuring and tracking these metrics. As the saying goes, "What gets measured gets managed, and what gets measured gets done." By holding myself accountable to these benchmarks, I stayed focused and could make necessary adjustments along the way.

Measurement alone isn't enough; accountability plays a crucial role in long-term success. In the next section, I'll share how I built accountability into my process to stay committed and follow through on my goals.

Losing ninety pounds in 2020 was a major undertaking, but success didn't happen by chance. By this point in my journey, I had already built a strong foundation. I had the *mindset* to overcome obstacles, the *purpose* to stay motivated, a *clear vision* of my goal, and *specific targets* broken down into manageable steps. However, one final piece was essential: execution.

I didn't do this alone. I surrounded myself with a team that provided guidance, support, and accountability. My doctor and nutritionist helped me set the right benchmarks. I worked with a chiropractor and a fitness trainer to ensure I was staying on track physically. Each of these experts played a role in helping me measure my progress, track my milestones, and make necessary adjustments along the way.

Tracking and accountability were key to the successful execution of my goals. I had tracking systems in place to monitor my daily and weekly habits, ensuring I was consistently working toward my goals. There were inevitable setbacks, days when I fell off track or progress slowed. But because I had clarity on my *why*, I was able to refocus and continue forward.

In the end, I achieved my goal. I lost weight, improved my health markers, and, more importantly, developed the habits necessary to sustain long-term progress. Years later, I continue to use the same principles to sustain my health and well-being.

You can do the same. With the right mindset, purpose, vision, goals, and execution system, any goal is within reach. When you establish the right disciplines and stay committed, real transformation happens.

I achieved this goal and others by using a system that helped ensure success. This method was developed over years of learning and practice. From losing weight to reaching financial goals, starting and growing multiple businesses, and pursuing other personal endeavors, I simplified concepts to help others achieve their goals. I call it the Personal Success System.

This book is designed to provide what other resources on self-improvement lack: a comprehensive, holistic system for turning your vision into sustained achievement. While some books may offer to help you define a purpose, set goals, and build habits, few offer an integrated approach that connects these pieces into a cohesive, actionable plan for success. This book fills that void. It's not just about setting goals or developing habits; it's about building your PSS to achieve meaningful, lasting success in every area of life.

WHY A SYSTEM MATTERS

Let's start with a hard truth. The world is awash with tools, frameworks, and strategies, yet many of us still feel stuck. We plan, hope, and dream, but we often fall short of our goals. Why? Because tools and frameworks alone aren't enough. Without a system that aligns your actions, mindset, and habits with your long-term vision, even the best tools become scattered and ineffective. Think of it like building a house. You might have the best materials and tools available, but without a blueprint and a step-by-step plan, your dream home will remain a dream.

Your PSS is that blueprint. It's the process of focusing your mindset, clarifying your purpose, developing a vision for a better future, then translating that vision into clear goals and idea initiatives, and developing them into a plan for execution and success. It's a step-by-step guide to ensure you don't just plan your success; you execute it. With this system, you'll stop reacting to life's demands and start intentionally designing the life you want.

HOW ADHD BUILT THIS SYSTEM

I was 43 years old when I was diagnosed with ADHD. Suddenly, countless struggles and frustrations from the past made perfect sense. Throughout my life, I'd constantly battled with starting exciting projects but rarely seeing them through to completion. I found myself brimming with ambitious ideas and inspiring goals, yet I consistently stumbled when trying to translate those dreams into tangible results.

Learning about ADHD was like turning on a light switch in a dimly lit room. It illuminated the reasons behind my past patterns of behavior: why my attention wandered, why mundane tasks seemed overwhelmingly difficult, and why, despite my best intentions, many of my objectives remained incomplete.

Over the years, I was frustrated that I was unable to bring my ideas to fruition or complete my goals. Not knowing that ADHD was at the root of these issues, I immersed myself in reading, pursued extensive training, and practiced diligently. Gradually, I built frameworks, strategies, and accountability mechanisms tailored to overcome my natural tendencies. These solutions became not only coping mechanisms but empowering tools.

Today, these very systems form the core of the PSS outlined in this book. I created them out of necessity to overcome my challenges. Now, I share them with you in the hope that they will help you break free from the habits and mindsets holding you back, empowering you to achieve the clarity and success you've been seeking.

THE FOUNDATION OF THIS BOOK

The PSS draws inspiration from proven methodologies found in numerous books, articles, resources, and personal experiences developed over time. This book goes further, integrating these concepts into a singular framework that you can apply to every area of your life. It's designed for busy professionals, entrepreneurs, students, and anyone striving to balance faith, family, fitness, work, friendships, and fun. Regardless of where you are in life, this system can help you clarify your vision, take meaningful action, and sustain momentum over the long haul.

The Personal Success System is a simple, actionable, and effective system to help you gain clarity and achieve your goals. It is designed to help you draft your own method that works for you and leads to your desired growth and outcomes. From vision-setting exercises to goal-tracking charts, you'll find everything you need to build and maintain your PSS.

> **THE PERSONAL SUCCESS SYSTEM IS A SIMPLE, ACTIONABLE, AND EFFECTIVE SYSTEM TO HELP YOU GAIN CLARITY AND ACHIEVE YOUR GOALS.**

THE PERSONAL SUCCESS SYSTEM

The five components of your Personal Success System are:

1. **Mindset:** Learn how to cultivate a growth mindset, rewire limiting beliefs, and establish transformational thinking to win the mental battle that precedes external success.
2. **DNA:** Craft your purpose and values to create a solid foundation for your life vision. This includes defining

your desired outcomes in key life areas, such as faith, fitness, family, focus, friends, and fun, and chunking these into actionable long-term goals.

3. **Vision:** Craft a personal vision for your life in the long term and the short term. This will inform the goals, habits, and actions you'll pursue to accomplish your vision.

4. **Goals:** Master practical tools and strategies for using the JACKED Framework™: setting goals and establishing daily and weekly habits to build momentum.

5. **Execution:** Discover how to track your progress, refine your goals, maintain accountability, and engage with resources to ensure consistent growth.

Throughout this book, you'll encounter powerful concepts and step-by-step strategies for transforming your life. To help you bring everything together and keep your journey on track, I've created the **Vision-Execution Snapshot**™, a single-page tool that captures your purpose, vision, goals, and daily habits all in one place. By the end, you'll have your own personalized snapshot to guide your actions, keep your big dreams in focus, and make disciplined execution a daily reality.

As you journey through these pages, remember that success is not a single moment or achievement; it's a process—the daily, intentional practice of aligning your actions with your vision and values. This book is your guide to that process. Let's build your PSS together and finally achieve the life you've always envisioned.

BUILDING YOUR WINNING PERSONAL SUCCESS SYSTEM

THE VISION-EXECUTION SNAPSHOT

When it comes to personal growth and high achievement, clarity is everything. You can have the purest intentions, the loftiest dreams, and a deep desire to succeed—but if your goals and priorities are vague or buried in a notebook somewhere, they'll get pushed aside by the whirlwind of daily life. Emails, errands, interruptions, and unexpected "urgent" problems will steal your focus before you even realize you've drifted. Without a clear, accessible plan to keep your purpose and priorities front and center, you'll find yourself working hard but moving in circles, never gaining the traction you truly want.

That's where the Vision-Execution Snapshot comes in. This isn't just another motivational tool; it's the ultimate clarity weapon. A one-page, high-impact summary of your Personal Success System, it keeps your *why*, your priorities, and your next actions visible, actionable, and alive. It's your personal playbook for life—the single page that distills everything you've built throughout this book: your mission, your values, your big-picture vision, your measurable goals, and your daily habits. This is the piece that takes all the work you've done so far and transforms it from an idea in your head into a compass you can hold in your hand.

When you keep your Snapshot where you can see it—on your desk, in your planner, on your phone's home screen, or even taped to your bathroom mirror—you turn your vision into a constant, unavoidable reminder. On the days when life hits hard, it's your rallying cry: *"This is why I started."* On the days when you're tempted to procrastinate, it's the steady hand that pulls you back on track. And on the days when you're winning, it's your scoreboard, showing you exactly how far you've come and where you're headed next. Over time, it becomes more than a piece of paper; it becomes your Personal Success Compass, always pointing you toward purpose-driven action.

Most people fail to reach their potential not because they lack skill, talent, or even discipline; it's because they drift. Without a clear, visible framework, they forget their *why*, they stop tracking their *how*, and before long, they're reacting to life instead of directing it. The Vision-Execution Snapshot solves that problem in one powerful way: it makes your vision visible and your next actions unmistakably clear.

Clarity fuels motivation. Visibility fuels execution. Combine those two, and you have momentum—and momentum is the secret weapon of high achievers. Think of the Snapshot like a dashboard for your life. In a car, you would drive blind without a speedometer, fuel gauge, or GPS. In life, your Snapshot gives you that same instant read on your direction, fuel levels (motivation), and course corrections. On tough days, it's your rallying cry. On the distracted days, it's your refocusing tool. On victorious days, it's your scoreboard.

In the coming pages of this book, we'll work together to develop each of the 9 Elements of the Vision-Execution Snapshot™. We'll walk step-by-step through defining your mission, clarifying your values, painting your long-term vision, setting specific annual and quarterly goals, and building the daily habits that turn those goals into reality. By the time you've completed this process, you'll not only have a finished Snapshot—you'll have the clarity, conviction, and structure to live it every single day.

Your Snapshot isn't a vague vision board; it's a tight, disciplined, practical roadmap. Every element has a purpose.

1. **Personal Mantra:** A short, memorable phrase that re-centers you in moments of stress or doubt. Examples: *"I do hard things." "Progress over perfection." "Purpose over comfort."*
2. **Personal Mission Statement:** A clear declaration of your purpose—the big *why* that drives everything. This should answer: *"What am I ultimately here to do, and why does it matter?"*
3. **Core Values:** Your non-negotiable principles. These act as filters for every decision. If an opportunity violates a core value, it's not worth pursuing.
4. **10-Year Vision:** The bold, long-term picture of your life when you've fully stepped into your potential. Describe it vividly: What does a Tuesday morning look like 10 years from now? Who are you with? What are you working on?
5. **3-Year Vision Picture:** A vivid, motivating, short-term future that feels tangible and exciting. This is your bridge between the long-term dream and the present.

6. **1-Year Goals:** Specific, measurable wins for the year—what "success" will look like 12 months from now. Keep these focused.

7. **Quarterly Goals:** Break your yearly goals into 90-day sprints. These milestones make big goals bite-sized and achievable.

8. **Weekly and Daily Habits:** The micro-actions that drive your macro-results. These are the behaviors that turn goals into reality—things like your morning routine, exercise, reflection time, and business prospecting.

Creating your Snapshot is only step one. Its power comes from living with it. Whether in your morning routine or during a midday check-in, look at it daily so that it becomes second nature. Revisit quarterly. Life changes, goals evolve, and circumstances shift. Every ninety days, update your Snapshot to reflect where you are now and where you're headed next. Let it call you out. When you're tempted to drift into busywork or self-sabotage, let your Snapshot be the voice that says, *"This is not the plan."* Share it selectively. Consider showing your Snapshot to an accountability partner, coach, or mastermind group. A shared vision creates higher commitment.

If you study top performers in business, sports, or creative arts, you'll notice a pattern: they all have some version of a clear, written, and visible plan. Elite athletes carry playbooks and visualize their game plan daily. CEOs use strategic dashboards to track progress in real-time. Writers keep their story outlines pinned above their desks. Your Vision-Execution Snapshot is your personal playbook for life. It's not wishful thinking; it's actionable clarity.

Take the time to build your Snapshot with complete honesty. Don't write what you think you *should* want—write what actually lights you up and aligns with your purpose. Once built, guard it fiercely. Life will try to bury it under noise, obligations, and other people's agendas. Refuse to let that happen. Keep it visible. Keep it relevant. Keep it yours.

Over time, you'll notice something powerful: the more you use your Snapshot, the less you'll have to wonder, *"What should I be doing right now?"* You'll know. And you'll be doing it. Because when you combine a clear vision with relentless execution, you don't just make progress—you close the gap between who you are and whom you were meant to be.

And that, my friend, is how you quit jacking around.

Let's get started building your PSS.

Scan To Download the Vision-Execution Snapshot™ Tool

PART 1

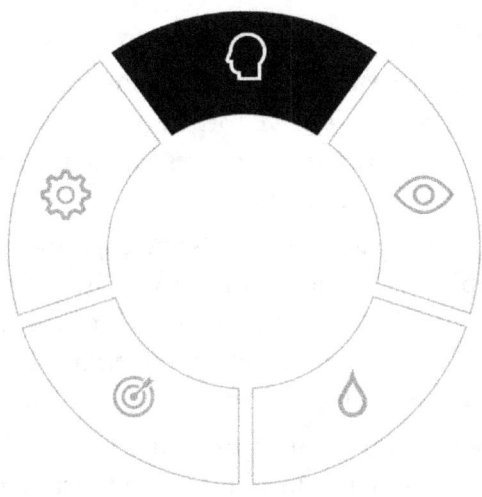

MINDSET

Mindset shapes how you interpret challenges, opportunities, and your own potential. It directs your reactions, fuels resilience, and influences every decision you make. Strengthening your mindset creates clarity, confidence, and stability, allowing you to move forward with purpose and conviction.

You can let circumstances define you, or you can step up and define your circumstances. The choice is yours.

> In this section, we'll lay the foundation for your personal growth by focusing on three essential elements:
>
> - Developing a growth and abundance mindset: The belief that abilities and intelligence can be cultivated through effort, and the conviction that opportunities and resources are plentiful if you are willing to seek them
> - Removing limiting beliefs and cognitive biases and replacing them with transformational thinking: Identifying the negative narratives that keep you stuck and reframing them into empowering stories that fuel your progress
> - Winning the war of the mind to unlock success: Cultivating mental resilience and focusing on overcoming setbacks and maintaining a clear vision of your goals
>
> Each of these principles will be brought to life through stories of athletes, leaders, and historical figures who overcame mental barriers to achieve greatness. Their journeys illustrate that success is not about being born with exceptional talent or privilege but about mastering the inner game of mindset.

The first component in the Personal Success System is Mindset. Mindset is where most goals fail. Having a growth mindset that equips people to overcome obstacles and challenges is required for growth. Most people aren't willing to step out of their comfort zone or change their current habits and activities.

Without possessing the mindset to grow, the rest of the system won't matter. A desire to grow will be present, but a few obstacles or inconveniences will end the growth process. If you can't win with the mindset, the rest of the PSS and this book won't matter.

Your current mindsets, habits, and actions have given you the results you have today. To achieve a better future and achieve

> **IF YOU CAN'T WIN WITH THE MINDSET, THE REST OF THE PSS AND THIS BOOK WON'T MATTER.**

your goals, these must change. Albert Einstein was famously credited with the quote, "Doing the same thing over and over and expecting different results is the definition of insanity."[15] So, to start your journey toward a better future, we must first determine what needs to change in your mindset and work to improve the clarity and effectiveness of your habits, actions, and systems of growth.

When I started my first company, I had no choice but to embrace a growth and abundance mindset, with a focus on winning the war in my mind. I was the single-income breadwinner for my family with three, now four, children. We didn't have a large backstop. Without possessing, fostering, and maintaining a growth mindset, I could have given in to the fear, doubt, anxieties, and negative brain messages that stop so many from pursuing and achieving their goals and ultimate success. I'm passionate, based on my successes and failures, about helping to instill a growth and abundance mindset in those I influence. Without these healthy mindsets, true success isn't possible.

1

PREPARING YOUR MIND FOR GROWTH

THE FOUR PRINCIPLES FOR PERSONAL GROWTH

Success isn't a matter of luck; it's the product of clarity, intention, and disciplined action. If you want to reach your fullest potential and implement the framework in this book, you must start with the right foundation. That foundation is built on four non-negotiable principles of personal growth. These principles are not vague concepts you simply "agree with" in theory; they are daily disciplines that shape your thinking, your behavior, and ultimately, your results. Without them, even the best strategies will fall flat. With them, you create the conditions for exponential growth.

Personal growth is not something that happens to you; it is something you step into with purpose. It's a process that requires self-honesty, deliberate effort, and the courage to push past comfort. Many people dream of becoming better versions of themselves, yet few are willing to truly examine where they are, take ownership of their growth, and do the hard work consistently. These Four Principles for Personal Growth™ are the guardrails and accelerators that will keep you moving toward your goals, even when the road gets rough.

Think of these principles as the "mental operating system" for your personal development. They will help you navigate setbacks, maximize opportunities, and avoid the common traps that cause people to stall or quit. When applied together, they will not only guide your mindset but also shape your actions and relationships so that every part of your life aligns with the person you're becoming. As you read, reflect on where you already excel in these principles and where you need to improve—because this isn't just information to know, it's a challenge to grow.

1. Self-Awareness: The Compass for Growth

Every journey begins with knowing where you are. Self-awareness is the foundation of all personal growth because you cannot change what you do not first acknowledge. This means taking an honest inventory of your circumstances, your wiring, your limiting beliefs, your strengths, and your weaknesses. Without it, you'll spend your energy moving in circles, chasing goals that don't truly matter, or running into the same walls over and over again. Self-awareness shines a light on both the obstacles holding you back and the opportunities waiting to be seized. It is the first step in designing a Personal Success System that is uniquely yours—and it's where clarity and transformation begin.

2. Ownership: Taking Full Responsibility for Your Growth

Growth does not happen by accident. No one can climb your mountain for you, and no one else can put in the daily work that growth requires. Taking ownership means refusing to outsource your success to circumstances, luck, or other people. It means embracing challenges instead of avoiding them, seeking out new knowledge, and making the choice every day to get better. When you own your growth, you stop waiting for permission or perfect conditions. You take action, you adapt, and you move forward—no matter what. Without ownership, personal growth is nothing more than wishful thinking.

3. Action: Turning Intentions Into Results

You cannot think, read, or plan your way into growth—you must act your way into it. Preparation is valuable, but action is essential. Theories and strategies only become transformation when they're tested in the real world. Growth happens when you start the project, have the hard conversation, take the class, make the call, or step into the unknown. Action brings clarity, builds confidence, and accelerates learning in ways that thinking alone never can. You don't need to have it all figured out—you just need to take the next step.

4. Trusted Relationships: The Multipliers of Growth

No one reaches their full potential in isolation. The right people accelerate your growth by providing accountability, encouragement, and perspective. Trusted relationships challenge you to rise higher, remind you of your vision when you lose sight of it, and walk with you through the hard seasons. These are not just casual acquaintances; they are like-minded, goal-oriented partners who share your values and push you toward your best. When you surround yourself with people who believe in you and expect more from you, you multiply your capacity for success.

By applying these four principles—self-awareness, ownership, action, and trusted relationships—you create a strong, sustainable foundation for personal growth. This is where your journey begins, and these principles will guide you as you build your Personal Success System, ensuring that your mindset, habits, and relationships align with your vision of success.

As you build a system to achieve success, it is important to define what success looks like for you. As it pertains to this book, here are some elements that you can use in defining success.

> **DEFINING SUCCESS**
>
> Success, as it pertains to the goals of this book, is not simply about financial wealth, career advancement, or external recognition, though these can be byproducts. True success is about designing a life aligned with your values, vision, and purpose. It is measured by:
>
> 1. Personal Fulfillment: Living a life that reflects your deepest values, passions, and beliefs
> 2. Consistent Growth: Progressing mentally, emotionally, and physically, continuously pushing beyond your limitations
> 3. Achieving Meaningful Goals: Setting and attaining goals that align with your long-term vision
> 4. Building Strong Relationships: Surrounding yourself with supportive, goal-oriented individuals who uplift and challenge you
> 5. Resilience and Adaptability: The ability to navigate challenges with a mindset that turns setbacks into stepping stones
> 6. Contribution and Impact: Using your success to help others, create positive change, and leave a meaningful legacy

> Success in this book is about becoming the best version of yourself, not by comparing yourself to others but by measuring your progress against your own potential. It's about being intentional with your time, energy, and actions so that you create a life of purpose and fulfillment.

With all these principles and thoughts in mind, we'll start our journey of building your PSS by changing your mindset and setting it on the course of success and fulfillment.

STOP MAKING EXCUSES

Excuses are the silent killers of progress. Every time you talk yourself out of taking the next step, you're choosing the familiarity of paralysis over the possibility of progress. Make no mistake, we are the best salespeople in the world at justifying our inaction. We craft explanations so convincing that even we start to believe them.

We say, "I intended to work out, but I was too tired." Meanwhile, we judge our friends and colleagues by what they accomplish, yet we judge ourselves by what we intended to do. The gap between intention and action is where excuses flourish.

The truth is this: growth requires discomfort. You can stay safe within your comfort zone and feel justified in not moving forward, or you can step into the unknown and feel the temporary sting of uncertainty. The question is, which discomfort are you willing to live with?

- **The Discomfort of Stagnation:** You feel frustrated with unfulfilled potential. You watch the opportunity pass. You know you could do more, but you don't. Over time, regret builds until it becomes harder to silence than any excuse.

- **The Discomfort of Growth:** You take risks. You stumble. You might fail, but each failure is a lesson that propels you closer to your goal. The temporary pain of change is nothing compared to the lasting satisfaction that comes with achievement.

Every time you catch yourself making an excuse, pause and ask: *Am I protecting my ego, or am I protecting my future?*

To quit jacking around, you must choose. You must commit to growth and success and stop settling for the easy path of excuses. When you decide to stop making excuses, you reclaim the power to shape your destiny. No more hiding behind good intentions. No more judging yourself by what you meant to do.

Decide today to step into the discomfort of growth. Decide to hold yourself accountable for action, not intention. When you do that, you'll find that the only thing holding you back isn't outside of you; it's the excuses you tell yourself. Now, you're done listening to them.

THE POWER OF INVESTING IN YOURSELF

A crucial truth separates those who experience lasting growth from those who stay stuck. Successful people make it a priority to invest in themselves. They devote time, energy, and often financial resources toward their own learning, development, and well-being. This isn't selfish; it's strategic. As you grow, so do your relationships, your work, and your influence.

Yet, many people hold back from investing in themselves. Sometimes it's due to fear or past disappointment. Maybe you once spent money on a program, course, or coach that didn't deliver what you hoped for. Maybe you feel guilty taking time for your own development when there are so many other demands. Or maybe you believe that investing in yourself is something "other people" do, people with more resources or fewer responsibilities. These are all limiting beliefs, and they're often what hold us back from the breakthrough we need most.

Growth always requires investment. You don't have to spend a fortune, but you do have to be intentional. That might mean carving out time each morning for focused reading or reflection, setting aside energy to learn a new skill, or enrolling in a class or coaching program that stretches you. It might mean buying the book, joining the mastermind, hiring the mentor, or even simply blocking off non-negotiable time for your personal goals. The point is, don't make excuses. Find a way to invest at a level you can manage, and commit to it.

Remember, every investment you make in yourself is a seed planted for your future. The results may not be immediate, but over time they compound, just like any wise investment. Don't let past failures or disappointments stop you. The greatest regret isn't money or time lost; it's the growth you forfeit when you refuse to invest in your own potential. Give yourself permission to make yourself a priority. When you do, you'll not only elevate your own life, but you'll also have more to give to everyone around you.

2

ESTABLISHING A WINNING MINDSET

Success in life starts in the mind. The way you think, what you believe about yourself, and how you frame your challenges all determine your trajectory. Your mindset is the lens through which you view the world, and it has the power to either propel you forward or hold you back. Think of a growth mindset as the engine that drives your potential. People with a growth mindset believe that failure is not the opposite of success but a stepping stone to learning and improvement. They embrace challenges, persevere when they face setbacks, and find inspiration in the success of others. Paired with an abundance mindset, the idea that there is more than enough success to go around, this way of thinking encourages collaboration, optimism, and a willingness to take risks.

Removing limiting beliefs is the next critical step. Limiting beliefs are often born from past experiences, cultural expectations, or fear of failure. These internal scripts tell us that we are not enough: not smart enough, not capable enough, or not deserving of success. The truth is, these beliefs are rarely grounded in reality. By identifying and challenging them, you can replace these thoughts with transformational ones that align with your goals and aspirations.

Finally, winning the war of the mind is about consistency and resilience. It's about training your mind to stay focused on your vision despite distractions and setbacks. It's about developing habits that reinforce positivity, gratitude, and growth. Your mental toughness determines how you respond when life throws challenges your way. Will you rise to the occasion, or will you retreat?

Remember that mindset is not a fixed trait; it's a muscle that can be strengthened with practice.

DEVELOPING A GROWTH AND ABUNDANCE MINDSET

A growth mindset is the belief that abilities and intelligence can be developed through effort and perseverance.[16] It is the foundation of all great achievements, fueling the determination to overcome obstacles and continuously improve. When combined with an abundance mindset, the belief that the world is full of opportunities and resources, this way of thinking becomes a powerful engine for personal and professional growth.

To gain a clearer perspective on a growth mindset, we can review one of the greatest athletes and one of the most successful female entrepreneurs of all time.

THE RELENTLESS DRIVE OF MICHAEL JORDAN

Michael Jordan's story is one of the most iconic examples of a growth mindset, resilience, and unwavering determination. As a teenager, Jordan faced one of his most significant setbacks when he did not earn a spot on his high school varsity basketball team. At the time, he was devastated, feeling the sting of rejection and doubt. Many would have taken this as a sign to give up, but Jordan chose a different path. Instead of letting failure define him, he used it as fuel to push himself further. This moment became a turning point in his life, igniting a relentless drive to prove himself.[17]

Determined to earn his place, Jordan didn't sulk or complain. He took immediate action, dedicating himself to improving every aspect of his game. He would wake up early before school to practice, spending hours shooting, dribbling, and refining his skills. His work ethic became legendary, often practicing longer and harder than anyone else around him. Jordan believed in the philosophy that "hard work beats talent when talent doesn't work hard." He made sure that no one would ever outwork him again.

Beyond physical practice, Jordan also worked on his mental toughness. He refused to let self-doubt control him and instead adopted a mindset of constant improvement. He visualized success, set high expectations for himself, and maintained an unwavering belief in his abilities. This mental fortitude enabled him to develop the resilience necessary to handle criticism, setbacks, and failures throughout his career.

When Jordan finally made the varsity team, he didn't just participate; he dominated. His hunger for excellence never faded. After high school, he went on to play at the University of North Carolina, where he led his team to a national championship in 1982 with a game-winning shot. His performance in college caught the attention of NBA scouts. In 1984, he was drafted by the Chicago Bulls as the third overall pick in the NBA draft.[18]

Once in the NBA, Jordan's legendary work ethic and drive only intensified. He approached every game with an insatiable desire to win, treating practice as seriously as championship games. He often reminded himself and others that talent alone wasn't enough; what separated the great from the legendary was the willingness to push past limits and continuously strive for improvement. Throughout his career, Jordan faced numerous obstacles, from early playoff disappointments to severe injuries. However, he never let setbacks deter him. Instead, he studied his weaknesses, adapted his strategies, and returned stronger each time.

One of Jordan's most famous quotes encapsulates his approach to success: "I've failed over and over and over again in my life and that is why I succeed."[19] He embraced failure as an essential part of growth, understanding that each missed shot and lost game provided a lesson that brought him closer to mastery. His ability to transform setbacks into stepping stones made him not just one of the greatest basketball players of all time but also a global icon who inspired millions to pursue excellence in their own fields.

Even after retiring from basketball, Jordan continued to embody the principles of resilience, discipline, and growth. His success extended into business, with his Jordan Brand becoming a billion-dollar empire, proving that the mindset that made him a champion on the court could be applied to any endeavor.

Michael Jordan's story serves as a powerful reminder that setbacks are not roadblocks but opportunities. His relentless drive, commitment to growth, and refusal to accept failure as a final result allowed him to set a standard for what is possible when one embraces a growth mindset. His legacy inspires athletes, entrepreneurs, and individuals worldwide to push beyond their limits and strive for greatness.

THE BOLD VISION OF SARA BLAKELY

Sara Blakely, the founder of Spanx®, is a powerful example of the growth and abundance mindset in action. Her path from a door-to-door fax machine seller to a self-made billionaire[20] is a testament to resilience, creative problem-solving, and an unwavering belief in her ability to succeed.

Before Spanx, Blakely faced a series of failures and rejections that could have discouraged even the most determined entrepreneur. She originally aspired to be a lawyer but failed the LSAT twice. Instead of dwelling on the setback, she pivoted and took a job as a fax machine salesperson, knocking on doors day after day. She was constantly met with resistance, rejection, and slammed doors. However, she developed a key skill during this time: handling rejection without taking it personally. She learned to turn every "no" into fuel for improvement, reframing resistance as feedback, rather than failure.

Blakely's idea for Spanx stemmed from a personal frustration: She wanted an undergarment that would provide a smooth look under white pants, but nothing on the market met her needs. Rather than accepting the status quo, she decided to create her own solution. The problem: She had no background in fashion, no knowledge of manufacturing, and only $5,000 in savings.[21] She did have an abundance mindset, the belief that obstacles were simply challenges to be solved.

Undeterred by her lack of experience, Blakely spent countless nights researching fabrics and learning about the production of hosiery. She visited textile mills and factories, only to be dismissed repeatedly. Industry experts told her that her idea wouldn't work. Some even laughed at her, but instead of letting these rejections stop her, she used them as motivation. She continued knocking on doors until she found a manufacturer willing to take a chance on her vision.

When she finally produced the first prototype, she faced yet another challenge: getting retailers to stock her product. Without connections in the fashion industry, she had to get creative. She personally pitched her product to department stores, often convincing buyers by demonstrating Spanx herself. One breakthrough moment came when a Neiman Marcus buyer agreed to try Spanx after Blakely demonstrated its effectiveness in the ladies' restroom. This unconventional approach worked; her product made it onto the shelves.

The real turning point came when Oprah Winfrey featured Spanx on her list of favorite things. Overnight demand skyrocketed. Blakely had no traditional marketing budget, so she relied on word of mouth, hustle, and her ability to connect with people. She personally packed and shipped orders, making sure every customer had the best experience possible.

Even as her business grew into a billion-dollar empire, Blakely continued to embrace the principles of a growth and abundance mindset. She reinvested in her company, kept learning, and sought out mentors to guide her through the complexities of running a global brand. She also prioritized giving back, creating The Sara Blakely Foundation (now known as The Red Backpack Foundation) to support female entrepreneurs and philanthropic initiatives.[22]

Blakely's story proves that success is not about having the perfect resume or the right connections. It's about resilience, creativity, and an unshakable belief that opportunities are everywhere if you are willing to seek them out and persist through challenges. Her bold vision transformed not only the fashion industry but also the way aspiring entrepreneurs view what is possible.

Taking inspiration from these real-world successes, you can begin to use the PSS tool for developing a growth and abundance mindset in your own life with the **GAIN Mindset Matrix™**.

THE GAIN MINDSET MATRIX

Grow. Adapt. Inspire. Navigate.

In the pursuit of lasting personal success, your mindset isn't just a contributing factor; it's the control panel for how you perceive, respond to, and create change. The GAIN Mindset Matrix is a proprietary framework designed to help you train your thinking for sustained growth, abundance, and resilience. Whether you're building a business, raising a family, shaping your legacy, or simply working to become the best version of yourself, your inner operating system must be optimized.

GAIN stands for Grow, Adapt, Inspire, and Navigate—four foundational mindset disciplines that multiply your capacity and momentum. Unlike passive affirmations or vague positivity, the GAIN Mindset is a dynamic, actionable model you can apply every day. When practiced consistently, it becomes the lens through which you see setbacks as setups, detours as data, and success as something meant to be shared, not hoarded.

Let's unpack each part of the matrix and show you how to activate it in your life.

G: GROW – EMBRACE CHALLENGES AS YOUR TRAINING GROUND

Growth doesn't come from reading about mindset or watching motivational videos. It comes from friction. From difficulty. From putting yourself in situations where you have no choice but to level up.

Michael Jordan wasn't always the best player on the court. In fact, being cut from his high school basketball team was one of the most formative events of his life. He didn't interpret it as rejection—he interpreted it as instruction. He used it as motivation to train harder, sharpen his skills, and become relentless in his pursuit of excellence. Likewise, Sara Blakely was rejected dozens of times by manufacturers who couldn't see her vision. But she didn't stop. She improved her pitch, refined her design, and remained steadfast through every "no" until she created a billion-dollar brand.

Growth-oriented people see challenges not as interruptions, but as invitations. They expect difficulty and welcome it. They understand that pressure creates diamonds—and discomfort is the price of breakthrough.

What holds most people back isn't a lack of skill; it's an unwillingness to struggle. The GAIN Mindset flips this. You become energized by resistance because you know it's sculpting your future strength.

How to Activate GROW:

- **Reframe problems as preparation.** Ask, *"What is this challenge equipping me for?"*
- **Develop discomfort tolerance.** Seek out situations that stretch you beyond your current capacity.
- **Keep a "growth journal."** Track challenges you've faced, what they taught you, and how you changed.
- **Remind yourself daily:** *Comfort never built anything worth remembering.*

A: ADAPT – PERSIST THROUGH SETBACKS AND SHIFT WITH PURPOSE

Adaptation is more than survival; it's strategic evolution. It's what turns temporary defeat into long-term domination.

Too often, people interpret failure as the end of the story. But those with a GAIN mindset see failure as the beginning of the next chapter. They understand that setbacks are not signs to stop but signals to adjust. In a 1997 Nike commercial, Michael Jordan said that he had missed over 9,000 shots, lost almost 300 games, and missed the game-winning shot 26 times.[23] Yet, these "failures" were the scaffolding for greatness. Sara Blakely's father celebrated her failures growing up, asking her what she had failed at each week. This reprogrammed her to see setbacks as successes in disguise.

Adaptation is not about bulldozing through obstacles. It's about learning fast, shifting wisely, and staying locked into your long-term vision. Those who adapt aren't reactive—they're proactive. They don't abandon the mission—they change the method.

Every success story has been written in edits. And those edits are made by people who are humble enough to learn and hungry enough to keep going.

How to Activate ADAPT:

- **Analyze your failures like a scientist.** What hypothesis didn't work—and why?
- **Ask yourself:** *"Is this a closed door or a call to reroute?"*
- **Keep your vision fixed, but your strategies flexible.**
- **Build resilience rituals.** After every loss, pause, reflect, adjust, and reengage.
- **Affirm:** *"I don't fail—I reframe."* Then get back to work with new data and renewed energy.

I: INSPIRE – LEARN FROM THE WINS OF OTHERS WITHOUT COMPARISON

Success leaves clues. But if you're operating from a scarcity or fixed mindset, you'll miss them. You'll see others' victories as a threat instead of a trail.

Inspiration is fuel, not a threat.

When Michael Jordan studied legends like Julius Erving and Magic Johnson, he wasn't intimidated—he was informed. He borrowed techniques, work ethic, and mindset cues. Sara Blakely surrounded herself with mentors, followed the journeys of resilient entrepreneurs, and let their breakthroughs become her playbook.

The GAIN Mindset doesn't get jealous; it gets curious. It asks, *"What can I learn from their path?"* rather than *"Why them and not me?"*

When you shift from envy to empathy and curiosity, you unlock accelerated growth. You begin to model excellence instead of resenting it. You adopt habits, ideas, and perspectives that would have taken years to develop on your own.

How to Activate INSPIRE:

- **Create a "Success Audit."** Who inspires you, and what are they doing that you can study or adopt?
- **Turn your social feed into a learning platform.** Follow high performers who stretch your thinking.
- **Flip comparison into collaboration.** Reach out to people doing what you want to do and learn from them.
- **Start asking "how?" instead of "why?"** How did they build what they built? How can I apply that insight today?
- **Surround yourself with possibility.** The more you see what's achievable, the more you'll believe you can achieve it, too.

N: NAVIGATE – BELIEVE IN UNLIMITED POTENTIAL AND SEEK NEW PATHS

Navigation is about more than movement; it's about belief. It's the ability to move forward with faith that opportunity is not finite and that your best days are not behind you.

Scarcity says success is a pie with only a few slices. Abundance says we can bake more pies.

Sara Blakely didn't invent shapewear—she innovated it. She entered a crowded industry and found whitespace because she *believed* there was more to be discovered. Jordan didn't just play basketball—he redefined it. They each navigated with boldness, knowing there was room for their version of excellence.

The GAIN Mindset is allergic to limitation thinking. It thrives on the idea that if something doesn't exist yet, it's an invitation to create it. Where others see competition, you see collaboration. Where others see lack, you see leverage.

Believing in unlimited potential is not about being naïve; it's about being creative. It's the foundation of innovation, invention, and reinvention.

How to Activate NAVIGATE:

- **Practice radical gratitude.** Gratitude trains your brain to see what's possible, not just what's missing.
- **Adopt an opportunity-seeking lens.** Ask yourself daily: *What door is trying to open today?*
- **Build instead of battle.** Focus on adding value, not "beating" the competition.
- **Visualize your life from the end.** Navigate today with the destination in mind.
- **Invest in collaboration.** The more you help others succeed, the more doors open for everyone—including you.

LIVE THE GAIN MINDSET MATRIX DAILY

The GAIN Mindset Matrix isn't a concept to admire; it's a system to activate.

These four disciplines—**Grow, Adapt, Inspire, and Navigate**—will transform the way you respond to adversity, interact with others, and see your future.

> When you **Grow**, you get stronger through challenge.
>
> When you **Adapt**, you remain grounded yet flexible.
>
> When you **Inspire**, you absorb greatness instead of resisting it.
>
> When you **Navigate**, you steer toward abundance instead of scarcity.

This is how winning thinkers move. This is how successful people keep rising. And this is how you quit jacking around—and start gaining ground.

Once you GAIN your mindset, a game-changing next step is to **Elevate** it.

WHY ADD "ELEVATE"?

While Grow, Adapt, Inspire, and Navigate help you optimize your internal operating system, **Elevate** shifts the mindset *outward*. It's about contribution. Expansion. Multiplication. This is the *abundance in action* pillar.

True success isn't just about what you *gain;* it's about what you *give*.

The Elevate mindset recognizes that the fastest way to grow is to lift others. Whether through mentoring, encouraging, teaching, serving, or leading, your mindset becomes stronger when it moves beyond you. Take a closer look at the Elevate mindset.

Core Belief: The more I help others rise, the more we all win.

Core Behavior: I look for ways to serve, share, and multiply what I know.

Power Prompt: "Who can I help rise today—and how?"

Examples of Elevate in Action:

- Michael Jordan mentored younger players and used his platform to inspire millions.
- Sara Blakely gave away $5 million to support women-led businesses during the COVID-19 pandemic.
- You don't need millions or a title—you just need a mindset that asks, *"Who can I serve with what I've gained?"*

How to Activate ELEVATE:

- **Mentor someone behind you.** Offer encouragement or insight you wish you had at their stage.
- **Document your journey.** Share your process so that others can benefit from your growth curve.
- **Contribute to a cause bigger than yourself.** Generosity recalibrates your mindset for abundance.

- **Practice daily acts of service.** Even small efforts (a helpful email, a kind word, a referral) amplify impact.
- **Live as a force multiplier.** What you've learned, overcome, and built can unlock others.

WHY THIS MATTERS

When you lift others, you rise too.

Elevate cements the transformation from self-focused growth to purpose-driven legacy. This is where mindset becomes movement—your influence expands because your intention has matured from *getting* to *giving*.

CULTIVATING YOUR GROWTH AND ABUNDANCE MINDSET

Building these mindsets requires daily practice and intentional effort. Growth and abundance are not just philosophies but habits, ways of thinking, and ways of acting that must be reinforced consistently. The more you practice these principles, the more naturally they will become part of your mindset. Here are the steps to cultivate a growth and abundance mindset to help you develop them.

1. **Reframe Failure:** Failure is not an indication of personal inadequacy; it is feedback, a guidepost on the road to success. Every great achiever has faced failure, but what sets them apart is their ability to reframe setbacks as stepping stones.

   Consider Thomas Edison's statement: "I have not failed. I've just found 10,000 ways that won't work."[24] Instead of allowing failure to deter him, he viewed it as a necessary step toward innovation. Similarly, Michael Jordan has spoken candidly about the many shots he missed and games he lost, acknowledging that those very failures paved the way for his greatness.

How to Apply This Principle

- When facing a setback, ask yourself, *"What can I learn from this experience?"*
- Keep a journal of lessons learned from mistakes and how they have helped you improve.
- Replace self-criticism with self-reflection. Analyze what went wrong so you can adjust your strategy.

2. **Seek Feedback:** Growth requires insight, and insight often comes from external perspectives. Constructive criticism is a valuable tool for improvement, yet many people avoid it out of fear or pride. A growth mindset welcomes feedback, seeing it as a tool for refinement rather than an attack on ability.

Bill Gates once said, "We all need people who will give us feedback. That's how we improve."[25] Successful leaders, athletes, and entrepreneurs actively seek advice and critique to refine their skills and strategies.

How to Apply This Principle

- Actively seek feedback from mentors, peers, and professionals.
- Instead of reacting defensively, ask clarifying questions to fully understand the feedback.

- Implement feedback into your daily practices and measure improvement over time.

3. **Practice Gratitude:** An abundance mindset thrives on gratitude. Rather than focusing on what you lack, shift your attention to the opportunities, resources, and people you have in your life. Studies have shown that practicing gratitude increases overall happiness, reduces stress, and improves resilience.[26]

Sara Blakely attributes much of her success to gratitude. She writes down things daily she is grateful for, reinforcing her belief in abundance and possibility.

How to Apply This Principle

- Keep a gratitude journal and list three things you are grateful for each day.
- When facing a challenge, reframe it by acknowledging the resources and support available to you.
- Express appreciation to those who help you along your journey: mentors, colleagues, family, and friends.

4. **Take Risks:** Growth and comfort cannot coexist. Those who achieve extraordinary success do so by stepping outside their comfort zones and taking calculated risks. Fear of failure often stops people from reaching for their dreams, but true progress only happens when you stretch beyond familiar territory.

Elon Musk took enormous risks launching Tesla and SpaceX, ventures that many believed were doomed to fail. Yet, his willingness to take bold chances allowed him to revolutionize the automotive and space industries.

How to Apply This Principle

- Start small. Take minor risks that push you slightly beyond your comfort zone.
- Embrace the discomfort of uncertainty; remind yourself that growth happens in the unknown.
- Reframe risk as an opportunity rather than a threat.

5. **Learn Continuously:** One of the defining traits of a growth mindset is the pursuit of knowledge. The most successful individuals understand that learning never stops. Whether it's reading books, attending workshops, taking courses, or surrounding themselves with inspiring people, continuous learning fuels growth and innovation.

Warren Buffett, one of the world's most successful investors, spends 80 percent of his day reading. He attributes much of his success to his commitment to lifelong learning. Similarly, Oprah Winfrey is known for her voracious reading habits and continuous pursuit of personal development.

How to Apply This Principle

- Set aside time each day for learning, whether through books, podcasts, courses, or mentorship.
- Surround yourself with people who challenge and inspire you.

- Be open to new ideas and perspectives, even those that contradict your current beliefs.

By consistently practicing these principles—reframing failure, seeking feedback, practicing gratitude, taking risks, and learning continuously—you will cultivate a mindset that fosters growth and abundance. This approach will not only accelerate your personal and professional development but also unlock opportunities you never thought possible.

WHY THESE MINDSETS MATTER

The stories of Michael Jordan and Sara Blakely demonstrate that success is not about avoiding failure, but how you respond to it. A growth and abundance mindset shifts your focus from limitations to possibilities, unlocking the potential to achieve goals that were once thought to be out of reach. By embracing these principles, you can transform challenges into opportunities and achieve remarkable success in any area of life.

3

COGNITIVE BIASES

HOW MENTAL SHORTCUTS SABOTAGE GROWTH—AND WHAT TO DO ABOUT IT

No matter how disciplined, driven, or well-intentioned we are, every one of us has blind spots—mental shortcuts that shape how we interpret the world, make decisions, and react to challenges. These are called *cognitive biases*, and they're wired into the way our brains process information. While they once helped our ancestors survive by reacting quickly to threats, they often undermine us in modern life by distorting our thinking and keeping us stuck in outdated patterns.

If you've ever clung to a failing plan because of how much time you already invested, ignored critical feedback that didn't match your self-image, or assumed everyone else saw things your way, you've experienced a cognitive bias in action. These mental habits can quietly sabotage progress and growth, especially when left unchecked. The good news? Once you recognize them, you can challenge them and rewrite the script. This chapter unpacks 12 of the most common cognitive biases that block personal and professional transformation, along with practical mindset shifts to overcome them. Because you can't build a winning Personal Success System on a faulty foundation, you must start with clear thinking.

> ## DEFINITION OF COGNITIVE BIASES
>
> Cognitive biases are systematic patterns of deviation from rationality in judgment and decision-making.[27] They occur when the brain processes information in a way that leads to subjective interpretations rather than objective analysis. These biases are often unconscious and stem from mental shortcuts (heuristics), personal experiences, emotions, or social influences.

Cognitive biases can significantly hinder personal growth by distorting perception, decision-making, and self-awareness. Here are twelve of the most impactful biases that prevent growth.

1. **Confirmation Bias:** Seeking out information that confirms existing beliefs while ignoring contradictory evidence, leading to stagnation and resistance to new perspectives.
2. **Dunning-Kruger Effect:** Overestimating one's own knowledge or ability, preventing learning and improvement due to false confidence.
3. **Negativity Bias:** Focusing more on negative experiences or feedback rather than positive ones, which can discourage risk-taking and personal development.
4. **Status Quo Bias:** Preferring things to stay the same rather than embracing change, leading to missed opportunities for growth.

5. **Sunk Cost Fallacy:** Continuing with a failing course of action due to past investments (time, money, effort) rather than pivoting toward better opportunities.
6. **Self-Serving Bias:** Attributing successes to internal factors (skills, effort) but blaming failures on external circumstances, which prevents learning from mistakes.
7. **Survivorship Bias:** Focusing only on success stories while ignoring failures leads to unrealistic expectations and misjudging the path to success.
8. **Projection Bias:** Assuming others think, feel, or value things the same way we do, limiting personal growth by reducing adaptability and empathy.
9. **Anchoring Bias:** Relying on the first piece of information seen, preventing flexible thinking and better decision-making.
10. **Framing Effect:** Making decisions based on how information is presented and not on the actual facts, leading to poor judgment.
11. **Recency Bias:** Emphasizing recent experiences over historical trends, which can lead to impulsive decisions and short-term thinking.
12. **Availability Heuristic:** Overestimating the information that is most readily available (such as personal experiences or media coverage), rather than relying on objective analysis.

Moving past these biases requires self-awareness, a willingness to challenge assumptions, and actively seeking diverse perspectives. Which of these do you think impacts you or those you work with the most?

ADDRESSING COGNITIVE BIASES

Recognizing and addressing cognitive biases is crucial for achieving personal and professional growth. By being aware of these biases, we can make more objective decisions, embrace constructive criticism, and develop a mindset of continuous improvement. Overcoming biases fosters adaptability, allowing individuals to be open-minded and willing to learn. This self-awareness leads to better relationships, improved decision-making, and a greater ability to reach personal goals. By intentionally challenging biased thinking, people can unlock their full potential and create meaningful progress in their lives.

Here's a breakdown of each cognitive bias with a common example and a transformative mindset truth to help overcome it.

1. **Confirmation Bias**
   - *Example:* John believes he is a great leader and only listens to feedback that praises him while ignoring constructive criticism.
   - *Transformative Mindset Truth:* "Growth comes from seeking truth, not validation. Challenge your beliefs regularly to uncover blind spots."

2. **Dunning-Kruger Effect**[28]
   - *Example:* A novice entrepreneur assumes they know everything about business just because they read a few books, leading to poor decisions.
   - *Transformative Mindset Truth:* "The more you learn, the more you realize how much you don't know. Stay humble and always seek improvement."

3. **Negativity Bias**
    - *Example:* Lisa receives ten compliments about her work but dwells on the one critical comment, causing self-doubt.
    - *Transformative Mindset Truth:* "Negative feedback is an opportunity for refinement, not a definition of worth. Focus on progress, not perfection."

4. **Status Quo Bias**
    - *Example:* Mark stays in a job he dislikes because he fears change, even though better opportunities exist.
    - *Transformative Mindset Truth:* "Growth begins at the edge of comfort. Embrace change as the gateway to new possibilities."

5. **Sunk Cost Fallacy**
    - *Example:* Sarah continues investing time in a failing project because she's already spent so much effort on it.
    - *Transformative Mindset Truth:* "Past effort does not dictate future success. The best choice is the one that serves your long-term vision."

6. **Self-Serving Bias**
    - *Example:* Tom takes full credit when a team project succeeds but blames others when it fails.
    - *Transformative Mindset Truth:* "Accountability is the foundation of growth. Own your mistakes, learn from them, and become better."

7. **Survivorship Bias**
    - *Example:* Emily sees a successful entrepreneur and assumes she can succeed the same way without realizing how many others failed.
    - *Transformative Mindset Truth:* "Success leaves clues, but so does failure. Learn from both to make informed decisions."

8. **Projection Bias**
    - *Example:* A manager assumes their employees are motivated by the same incentives as they are, leading to disengagement.
    - *Transformative Mindset Truth:* "Everyone has a unique perspective. Seek to understand rather than assume."

9. **Anchoring Bias**
    - *Example:* Alex sees a product initially priced at $1,000, then discounted to $700, assuming it's a great deal without evaluating alternatives.
    - *Transformative Mindset Truth:* "Never base decisions on the first number you see. Gather multiple perspectives before concluding."

10. **Framing Effect**
    - *Example:* A fitness plan marketed as "90 percent success rate" sounds better than "10 percent failure rate," even though both mean the same thing.
    - *Transformative Mindset Truth:* "Truth doesn't change with perspective. Train yourself to look beyond the frame and see the full picture."

11. **Recency Bias**
    - *Example:* An investor panics and sells their stocks because of a recent market drop, ignoring historical trends.
    - *Transformative Mindset Truth:* "Short-term fluctuations don't define long-term success. Look at the bigger picture before reacting."

12. **Availability Heuristic**
    - *Example:* A person refuses to fly because of a recent plane crash on the news, despite air travel being statistically safer than driving.
    - *Transformative Mindset Truth:* "What's most visible isn't always most accurate. Make decisions based on facts, not fears."

FINAL THOUGHT ON COGNITIVE BIASES

By recognizing these biases and adopting the right mindset, you can break free from limitations and unlock greater personal and professional growth. Which of these resonates with you the most?

4

TRANSFORMATIONAL THINKING

Transformational thinking is the deliberate choice to replace limiting beliefs with empowering truths that expand what you believe is possible for your life. Limiting beliefs act like invisible chains—unseen but deeply felt—anchoring you to past failures, external opinions, or fears that masquerade as facts.

They whisper in your ear phrases like, *"I'm not good enough,"* *"I'll never be able to do that,"* or *"People like me don't succeed."* Over time, these thoughts feel less like opinions and more like reality, shaping your actions, decisions, and ultimately, your results. But here's the truth—these beliefs are rarely rooted in fact. They are simply stories we've told ourselves, and like all stories, they can be rewritten.

Breaking free from these mental barriers isn't just about positive thinking; it's about challenging the very assumptions you've been living by, replacing them with a mindset that opens doors instead of closing them.

Transformational thinking is about shifting from "I can't" to "I can," from "I've never" to "I will." It's the mental reset that allows you to see obstacles not as stop signs but as stepping stones. And when you reframe how you see yourself and the world around you, you open up space for breakthroughs you once thought were impossible. This shift often begins with one defining moment—an instance where you dare to question what everyone else accepts as a hard limit.

History is full of examples of people who refused to accept the so-called "impossible" as final. One of the most powerful illustrations comes from the world of athletics, where for decades an invisible wall stood in front of every runner on the planet: the four-minute mile. Scientists, coaches, and even athletes themselves believed it couldn't be done. It wasn't just a physical barrier—it had become a deeply ingrained mental one. And yet, in 1954, a young medical student named Roger Bannister decided to rewrite that story, proving to the world that the limits we accept are often the limits we've created.

THE STORY OF ROGER BANNISTER: BREAKING THE FOUR-MINUTE MILE[29]

For decades, it was commonly accepted that the four-minute barrier was a physiological impossibility, a limit that even the best runners in the world could not overcome.[30]

The belief was so strong that medical experts claimed attempting such a pace could be fatal, warning that the strain on the heart and lungs would be too great.[31] The very idea of breaking four minutes had become more than just a physical challenge; it was a deeply ingrained psychological barrier.

Enter Roger Bannister, a young medical student at the University of Oxford who refused to accept conventional wisdom. Bannister was not a full-time athlete; he balanced his training with his rigorous medical studies. Unlike other runners who focused purely on endurance and strength, Bannister understood the importance of the mind in performance. He believed that breaking the four-minute barrier was just as much a psychological challenge as it was a physical one.[32]

Bannister adopted a revolutionary approach, using scientific principles to optimize his training. He studied biomechanics, aerodynamics, and oxygen intake, meticulously crafting a plan that would allow him to push his body beyond its perceived limits. But more importantly, he conditioned his mind to believe that the impossible was possible. He visualized his success long before it became a reality. He saw himself crossing the finish line in record time and refused to let doubts creep into his mind.

On May 6, 1954, at the Iffley Road Track in Oxford, Bannister lined up for history. The weather conditions were far from ideal; strong winds and rain threatened to derail his attempt.[33] Many would have postponed, waiting for perfect conditions, but Bannister, understanding the power of mental resilience, chose to run anyway. With the help of two pacers, he set out on his historic run. As he crossed the finish line in three minutes and 59.4 seconds, the world stood in awe. He had shattered not only a long-standing athletic record but also a deep-rooted belief that had held athletes back for generations.

Bannister's achievement was not just a victory in sports; it was a victory of mindset over limitation. His success proved that mental barriers are often more restricting than physical ones.[34] What's even more astonishing is what happened next. Within just a few weeks of Bannister's record-breaking run, another runner broke the four-minute mile. In the years that followed, dozens of athletes achieved what was once thought to be impossible.

Today, running a sub-four-minute mile is a standard achievement for elite runners. Bannister's breakthrough demonstrated a fundamental truth. Once a limiting belief is shattered, it opens the floodgates for others to succeed.

Bannister's story is a perfect illustration of the principles in this book. His journey highlights the importance of:

1. **Challenging Limiting Beliefs:** Just because something has never been done before does not mean it is impossible. Bannister refused to accept conventional wisdom and instead focused on what *could* be done.
2. **The Power of Visualization:** By vividly imagining his success, Bannister trained his mind to believe in his potential, a key factor in achieving breakthrough results.
3. **Embracing Discomfort and Taking Action:** He didn't wait for perfect conditions; he trusted his preparation and stepped boldly into the challenge despite obstacles.
4. **Inspiring Others Through Action:** Once he broke the barrier, others quickly followed, proving that our own breakthroughs can help others achieve more than they ever thought possible.

Bannister's story teaches us that most of the barriers we face in life are not physical; they are mental. Whether in business, personal development, or athletic achievement, our beliefs shape our reality. When we redefine what is possible, we unlock a world of potential, not only for ourselves but for those who follow in our footsteps.

PRACTICAL STEPS TO TRANSFORM YOUR THINKING

Transforming your thinking is a deliberate and ongoing process. It requires breaking down mental barriers, rewiring your thought patterns, and taking these Practical Steps to Transform Your Thinking™ toward a growth-oriented mindset. Here's how you can do it.

1. IDENTIFY YOUR LIMITING BELIEFS

The first step in transforming your thinking is identifying the thoughts and beliefs that hold you back. Often, these are subconscious narratives that dictate our actions and decisions without us realizing it.

Take time to reflect on what you tell yourself daily. What excuses do you make? What fears creep into your mind when you think about pursuing your goals? Common limiting beliefs include:

- "I'm not talented enough."
- "I'll never be as successful as others."
- "I'm too old/too young to start."
- "Failure means I'm not capable."
- "I don't have enough resources to succeed."

Once you've identified these thoughts, write them down. The act of bringing them into the open helps you become aware of their influence. When you see them in writing, you may realize how irrational or untrue they really are.

2. CHALLENGE THE VALIDITY OF THESE BELIEFS

Now that you've identified your limiting beliefs, it's time to dismantle them. Ask yourself the following questions:

- Is this belief based on fact or fear?
- Do I have concrete evidence to support this belief?
- Have others in similar situations overcome this same challenge?
- What would happen if I chose to believe the opposite?

Most limiting beliefs are rooted in fear and assumptions rather than objective reality. By challenging their validity, you begin to see that they hold no real power over you. Replace them with statements that reflect your true potential. For example:

- Instead of "I'm not talented enough," say, "Talent is developed through practice, and I can improve with effort."
- Instead of saying, "I'll never be as successful as others," say, "My journey is unique, and I define my own version of success."

3. REFRAME YOUR NARRATIVE

The way you frame your experiences directly impacts your mindset. Instead of seeing setbacks as proof of failure, view them as necessary steps toward success.

Reframing your narrative means actively choosing empowering perspectives over self-defeating ones. For example:

- Instead of saying, "I've failed too many times to succeed," tell yourself, "Each failure is bringing me closer to my breakthrough."
- Instead of thinking, "I'm not good at this," say, "I'm learning and improving every day."
- Instead of believing, "I'm unlucky," reframe it as, "I create my own opportunities through effort and persistence."

When you reframe your thoughts, you start seeing opportunities where you once saw obstacles.

4. VISUALIZE YOUR SUCCESS

Visualization is a powerful tool used by top athletes, entrepreneurs, and high achievers to condition their minds for success. By creating a clear mental image of what you want to achieve, you reinforce positive expectations and train your brain to recognize opportunities that align with your vision.

Like Roger Bannister visualized himself breaking the four-minute mile before he actually did it, you can use visualization to program your mind for success. Here's how:

- **Close your eyes and picture yourself achieving your goal in vivid detail.** See the setting, feel the emotions, and imagine every step of the process.
- **Engage all your senses.** If your goal is to start a business, imagine shaking hands with your first customer, hearing the sound of success notifications, and feeling the pride of accomplishment.

- **Practice this daily.** The more consistently you visualize success, the more real it becomes in your mind, and eventually, in your reality.

5. SURROUND YOURSELF WITH POSITIVITY

Your environment greatly shapes your mindset. If you constantly expose yourself to negativity, doubt, and criticism, it will be much harder to maintain a growth-oriented perspective.

To cultivate a positive environment:

- **Spend time with people who inspire and support you.** Seek out mentors, coaches, or peers who encourage growth.
- **Limit exposure to negativity.** Avoid excessive time on negative news, social media comparison, or toxic relationships.
- **Engage with uplifting content.** Read books, listen to podcasts, and consume media that reinforce positive thinking and success-oriented habits.
- **Join communities that foster growth.** Mastermind groups, networking circles, or personal development forums can provide accountability and motivation.

By actively choosing your influences, you protect and strengthen your mindset against negativity.

6. USE POSITIVE AFFIRMATIONS AND MANTRAS

One of the most effective ways to rewire your mindset is through positive affirmations and mantras. By repeatedly affirming empowering beliefs, you train your brain to internalize new thought patterns and override negative self-talk. Affirmations can help counter cognitive biases and limiting beliefs, reinforcing your commitment to growth and success.

Here's how to incorporate them into your routine.

- **Choose affirmations that resonate with you.** Examples include:
    - "I am capable and confident in my abilities."
    - "I embrace challenges as opportunities to grow."
    - "Every setback is a setup for a comeback."
    - "I am in contro.l of my success and happiness."
- **Repeat them daily.** Say them in the morning, before bed, or anytime self-doubt creeps in.
- **Write them down.** Place them where you can see them: on your mirror, desk, or phone wallpaper.
- **Speak them with conviction.** The more emotion and belief you put behind your affirmations, the more powerful they become.

Over time, positive affirmations help reshape your subconscious beliefs, allowing you to act with confidence and determination.

7. TAKE ACTION

Transformation doesn't happen through thought alone; it requires action. You cannot change your mindset by merely hoping it will improve; you must engage in habits that reinforce the new way of thinking.

Here's how to take intentional action.

- **Set small, achievable goals that align with your new mindset.** If your limiting belief was, "I'm not good at public speaking," start by practicing in front of a mirror, then in front of a friend, and gradually increase your audience.
- **Track your progress.** Keep a journal of your mindset shifts and achievements. Documenting growth reinforces your belief in your ability to improve.
- **Push through discomfort.** Growth happens outside of your comfort zone. Take small risks that challenge your old beliefs and prove to yourself that change is possible.
- **Celebrate wins.** Acknowledge progress, no matter how small. Every step forward is evidence that transformation is happening.

By taking consistent action, your new way of thinking becomes ingrained in your identity, ultimately leading to lasting personal growth and success. Transforming your thinking isn't a one-time event; it's a lifelong commitment to growth. By identifying limiting beliefs, challenging them, reframing your narrative, visualizing success, surrounding yourself with positivity, using affirmations, and taking action, you create a mindset that propels you toward your fullest potential. Your thoughts shape your reality, and by mastering them, you unlock the door to unlimited possibilities.

WHY THIS MATTERS

Your beliefs shape your reality. By identifying and replacing limiting beliefs with transformational thinking, you unlock the door to new possibilities. The story of Roger Bannister shows that the only limits that truly exist are the ones we impose on ourselves. When you break free from these mental barriers, you create a foundation for achieving your greatest goals.

5

WINNING THE WAR OF THE MIND

The greatest battles you will ever fight won't take place in a boardroom, a courtroom, or even on a playing field—they will take place in your mind. Before you ever face an external challenge, you will first encounter an internal one: the doubts that whisper "you can't," the fears that tell you to turn back, and the temptations to settle for less than you're capable of. This is the war of the mind—a daily contest between belief and defeat, between clarity and confusion, between persistence and surrender. Your success in life will largely be determined by which side wins more often.

Mental resilience is not about pretending challenges don't exist; it's about facing them head-on with a clear purpose and an unshakable determination to keep moving forward. Life will hand you setbacks, rejections, and obstacles you didn't see coming. The question is not whether you'll encounter them, but whether you'll let them define you. Those who win the war of the mind understand that failure is not fatal, rejection is not final, and delay does not mean denial. They see every challenge as a training ground for strength, clarity, and innovation.

One of the clearest examples of this truth can be found in the grit of Thomas Edison. History remembers him as one of the greatest inventors of all time, but few realize how many times he fell short before achieving success. Edison himself once said, "I have not failed. I've just found 10,000 ways that won't work." To him, every unsuccessful attempt wasn't a verdict of failure; it was data, feedback, and a necessary step toward a breakthrough. And that perspective made all the difference.

THE GRIT OF THOMAS EDISON

> *I have not failed. I've just found 10,000 ways that won't work.*
> —Attributed to Thomas Edison

Thomas Edison, one of the greatest inventors in history, exemplified mental resilience, perseverance, and an unwavering commitment to innovation. His ability to push through failure and rejection is a testament to what it truly means to possess a growth mindset.

While many recognize Edison as the creator of the electric light bulb, fewer realize the incredible number of setbacks he encountered before reaching success. He reportedly failed over 1,000 times while attempting to develop a working electric light bulb.[35] Some accounts even claim the number was closer to 10,000, but for Edison, failure was never truly failure; it was data, feedback, and a necessary part of progress.

Edison's grit wasn't limited to just the light bulb. Over his lifetime, he accumulated over 1,000 patents,[36] many of which stemmed from years of trial and error. His work revolutionized industries such as telecommunications, sound recording, and power distribution. However, many of his ideas didn't take off immediately, or at all. Some inventions failed completely, while others took years to refine. His invention of the phonograph, for example, was initially met with skepticism and disbelief, with many experts dismissing it as a gimmick. Yet, Edison persisted, improving upon his designs until his vision became a reality.

REFRAMING FAILURE AS A STEPPING STONE

Edison's story teaches us that resilience is not about being impervious to failure but about seeing setbacks as temporary and necessary for growth. He didn't view his unsuccessful experiments as wasted effort; instead, he saw them as valuable learning experiences that brought him closer to a solution. When questioned about his repeated failures in developing the light bulb, he explained, "Every wrong attempt discarded is another step forward."[37]

This mindset is crucial for anyone striving to achieve big goals. Too often, people interpret failure as a sign that they're incapable or that their dreams are unattainable. Edison's approach reveals the opposite; failure is merely an indication that another approach is needed. His resilience demonstrates that every unsuccessful attempt holds the potential for learning and progress, provided one has the grit to persist.

LESSONS FROM EDISON'S GRIT AND PERSEVERANCE

Edison's unwavering commitment to his vision offers several key takeaways for anyone seeking success.

1. **Persistence outlasts talent.** While intelligence and skill are important, resilience is what separates those who

succeed from those who give up. Edison's genius wasn't just his ability to invent; it was his refusal to quit when faced with obstacles.

2. **Every failure provides insight.** Instead of viewing failures as roadblocks, Edison saw them as guideposts pointing him in the right direction. Every experiment that didn't work helped refine his approach and narrow down what would work.

3. **Vision is essential.** Without a clear vision, it's easy to become discouraged by setbacks. Edison kept his focus on the bigger picture, allowing him to push through temporary frustrations.

4. **Innovation requires risk.** Many of Edison's ideas were ahead of their time, and he faced criticism and skepticism. However, he was willing to take risks and challenge conventional wisdom, leading to groundbreaking discoveries.

APPLYING EDISON'S MINDSET TO YOUR OWN LIFE

Edison's story isn't just about inventing; it's about the power of grit in any endeavor. Whether you're building a business, mastering a skill, or pursuing a personal goal, adopting Edison's resilience can transform your approach to obstacles.

- When you encounter failure, ask yourself:
    - What can I learn from this experience?

- Stay committed to your long-term vision.
    - Progress often requires numerous iterations before success is achieved.

- Reframe setbacks as valuable data.
    - Each attempt gets you closer to discovering what works.
- Adopt a mindset of continuous learning and experimentation.
    - Success isn't about perfection; it's about refinement and persistence.

By embracing the lessons from Edison's grit, you can cultivate a mindset that sees failure not as an end but as a crucial step toward achieving breakthroughs. His perseverance didn't just change his own life; it changed the world, proving that those who refuse to give up are the ones who ultimately leave the biggest impact.

THE PERSEVERANCE OF J.K. ROWLING

Before J. K. Rowling became one of the wealthiest and most beloved authors of our time, she endured years of hardship, rejection, and self-doubt. Her story is one of resilience, persistence, and an unwavering belief in her vision.[38]

OVERCOMING EARLY STRUGGLES

J.K. Rowling's journey to success was anything but easy. In the early 1990s, she found herself at one of the lowest points in her life. She had recently gone through a painful divorce, was unemployed, and was struggling to raise her young daughter as a single mother. With no steady income and living on government assistance, she faced overwhelming financial insecurity.

Despite her circumstances, Rowling held onto her dream of becoming a published author. She had conceived the idea of *Harry Potter* years earlier while on a delayed train from Manchester to London, but bringing her vision to life proved to be a monumental challenge. She wrote the first draft of *Harry Potter and the Philosopher's Stone* in cafes, often with her daughter sleeping in a stroller beside her.[39] She had no guarantee of success, only a deep conviction that her story deserved to be told.

FACING REJECTION HEAD-ON

Once her manuscript was complete, Rowling sent it to multiple publishers, only to receive rejection after rejection. In total, 12 different publishing houses turned her down,[40] each dismissing her work as unmarketable or not suitable for a wide audience.

Many aspiring writers would have taken these rejections as a sign to quit, but Rowling refused to give up. She believed in her story, and more importantly, she believed in herself. She continued submitting her manuscript until one day, Bloomsbury, a small publishing house in London,[41] took a chance on her. Even then, the publisher advised her to get a day job, warning that she was unlikely to make a living as a children's author.[42]

THE BREAKTHROUGH MOMENT

Rowling's perseverance paid off in ways she never could have imagined. Once *Harry Potter and the Philosopher's Stone* hit the shelves, it became an instant sensation.[43] Readers of all ages fell in love with the story of the young wizard, and word of mouth spread rapidly. The book's popularity soared, leading to a bidding war for the U.S. publishing rights, which Scholastic won for an unprecedented $105,000, a life-changing sum for Rowling at the time.[44]

As the *Harry Potter* series grew in popularity, it became a global phenomenon, breaking sales records and inspiring a generation of readers. Rowling's once-rejected manuscript turned into one of the best-selling book series in history, selling over 500 million copies worldwide.[45] Her books were adapted into a blockbuster film franchise, theme parks, and an extensive merchandising empire, making her the first author to become a billionaire through writing.[46]

LESSONS FROM ROWLING'S RESILIENCE

Rowling's story teaches us invaluable lessons about perseverance, self-belief, and mental toughness. Her journey illustrates the importance of staying resilient and focused, even when the odds seem stacked against you. Here are some key takeaways from her experience.

1. **Rejection is not the end.** Rowling's manuscript was rejected 12 times, but she didn't allow those setbacks to define her. If she had stopped submitting after the first few rejections, the world might never have experienced *Harry Potter*. The key lesson: Rejection is often just a step on the path to success.
2. **Believe in your work.** Even when others doubted her, Rowling held onto her belief that her story was worth sharing. Confidence in your vision is crucial for success. If you don't believe in yourself, how can others be expected to believe in you?

3. **Persistence pays off.** Rowling kept pushing forward despite overwhelming difficulties. She didn't let financial struggles, single parenthood, or professional rejections stop her from pursuing her dream. Her persistence was the key to unlocking her success.
4. **Success often comes after hardship.** Rowling's life circumstances were far from ideal when she was writing *Harry Potter*, yet she used her struggles as fuel rather than letting them defeat her. Many of the most successful people have had to endure hardship before reaching their goals.

APPLYING ROWLING'S MINDSET TO YOUR OWN LIFE

Rowling's perseverance didn't just lead to her personal success; it has inspired millions of readers worldwide to believe in magic, in storytelling, and in their own ability to overcome adversity. If you are facing rejection, hardship, or doubt in your own journey, take inspiration from her story:

- **Don't let setbacks discourage you.** Every rejection is one step closer to the right opportunity.
- **Keep working on your craft.** Whether you are a writer, entrepreneur, or artist, persistence and continuous improvement are key.
- **Hold onto your vision.** If you truly believe in what you're creating, keep pushing forward until you find the right audience or opportunity.
- **Remember that success often comes after struggle.** Keep moving forward, even when things seem impossible.

J.K. Rowling's story is proof that perseverance, resilience, and unwavering self-belief can lead to extraordinary success, no matter how many obstacles stand in the way.

—⁂—

Drawing on the stories of Edison and Rowling, you can begin to develop practical Steps to Build Mental Resilience™. These steps will also help you take key steps in building your Personal Success System as we work through this book and its tools.

BUILDING MENTAL RESILIENCE: PRACTICAL STEPS

Mental resilience is the ability to bounce back from challenges, adapt to adversity, and persist through difficulties. It is not an innate trait but a skill that can be developed through intentional practice. Strengthening your resilience equips you to handle stress, setbacks, and uncertainty with confidence and determination. Here's how you can build a strong foundation for mental toughness.

1. DEVELOP CLARITY IN YOUR PURPOSE, VALUES, AND A COMPELLING VISION

A strong sense of purpose provides the foundation for resilience. Gaining clarity on your values and how you live your life is key to navigating your actions. When you have a clear vision of what you want to achieve, it becomes easier to stay focused and overcome obstacles you will face. The following chapters in this book will help you accomplish this.

- **Develop and write your goals.** Clarity is key. Define your short-term and long-term goals and keep them in a place where you can see them daily. You will develop these with clarity based on your purpose as you build your PSS.
- **Visualize success.** Imagine yourself overcoming challenges and reaching your goals. This mental exercise reinforces motivation and determination.
- **Break it down.** Large goals can feel overwhelming. Break them into smaller, achievable steps to maintain momentum and avoid discouragement.
- **Revisit and adjust.** At the same time as your life situations change, your goals should, too. You should review your vision regularly and make adjustments to stay aligned with your purpose.

2. EMBRACE SETBACKS AS LEARNING OPPORTUNITIES

Setbacks and failures are inevitable, but resilient individuals view them as valuable learning experiences rather than signs of defeat. Reframing setbacks as stepping stones to success helps cultivate perseverance.

- **Adopt a growth mindset.** You should believe that skills and abilities can be improved through effort and practice.
- **Analyze what went wrong.** Instead of dwelling on failure, break it down: What factors contributed? What can be improved next time?
- **Develop alternative strategies.** If one approach doesn't work, resilience means being flexible and trying another way.

- **Keep moving forward.** Don't let one setback define your entire journey. Acknowledge mistakes, adjust your approach, and keep pushing ahead.

3. PRACTICE MINDFULNESS AND GRATITUDE

Staying present and focusing on what you're grateful for can help reduce stress, build emotional resilience, and maintain a positive outlook in difficult times.

- **Incorporate mindfulness practices.** Meditation, deep breathing, or simply pausing to observe your surroundings can help center your mind and reduce stress.
- **Complete daily gratitude exercises.** Write down three things you're grateful for each day. This simple practice rewires your brain to focus on positivity rather than negativity.
- **Reframe negative thoughts.** When facing challenges, shift your perspective by asking, "What is one positive thing that can come from this situation?"
- **Engage in activities that bring joy.** Doing things that bring fulfillment, whether reading, exercising, or spending time with loved ones, helps maintain emotional balance.

4. CULTIVATE SELF-COMPASSION

Self-compassion is essential for resilience. Treating yourself with kindness and understanding, especially during tough times, helps you recover from setbacks more quickly.

- **Avoid harsh self-criticism.** Speak to yourself as you would to a close friend. Replace negative self-talk with encouragement.
- **Acknowledge your efforts.** Recognize that effort matters just as much as outcomes. Progress is success.
- **Learn from failures without self-blame.** Rather than internalizing failure as a personal flaw, see it as part of the learning process.
- **Prioritize self-care.** Mental resilience is strengthened by physical and emotional well-being. Get enough sleep, eat nourishing foods, and engage in relaxation activities.

5. SURROUND YOURSELF WITH SUPPORT

Resilience does not mean facing hardships alone. A strong support system can provide encouragement, perspective, and accountability.

- **Build a circle of positive influences.** Surround yourself with people who uplift and inspire you, whether friends, mentors, or colleagues.
- **Seek guidance from mentors.** Learning from those who have navigated similar challenges can provide valuable insights and motivation.
- **Share your struggles.** Talking about difficulties with trusted individuals can provide emotional relief and practical solutions.
- **Reciprocate support.** Encouraging others and offering help in return strengthens relationships and fosters a community of resilience.

6. COMMIT TO CONTINUOUS IMPROVEMENT

Resilience grows when you see progress. Celebrating small victories and setting new challenges keeps you moving forward, even in difficult times.

- **Track your progress.** Keep a journal of your achievements, no matter how small. This reinforces confidence and motivation.
- **Set personal growth challenges.** Regularly push yourself to step outside your comfort zone and develop new skills.
- **Adapt and evolve.** Success isn't about avoiding failure but about learning and improving from each experience.
- **Celebrate wins.** Acknowledge accomplishments and use them as fuel to keep striving toward greater success.

By incorporating these practical steps, you can build resilience that allows you to thrive in the face of adversity. Resilient individuals don't avoid challenges; they embrace them, learn from them, and emerge stronger on the other side.

WHY WINNING THE WAR OF THE MIND MATTERS

The war of the mind is not a single battle; it is a lifelong series of choices to stay focused, adaptable, and positive. By cultivating mental resilience and maintaining clarity of purpose, you can navigate any obstacle and find success that is not only significant but also sustainable. The stories of Edison and Rowling remind us that resilience is a skill anyone can develop, and that it is the key to unlocking your true potential.

Stop waiting for life to happen. Take control.
Lead your circumstances before they lead you.

DEVELOPING YOUR PERSONAL MANTRA

In the PSS, your mindset is the engine that drives everything else forward. One of the most powerful tools you can put in your daily arsenal is a *personal mantra*—a short, potent phrase or verse that captures your highest values and reminds you who you're becoming. Repeating your mantra every morning (and whenever you need a mental reset) primes your brain for growth, abundance, and intentional action.

WHY A MANTRA MATTERS

- **Focuses Your Attention:** Your mind is like a race car; if you don't steer it toward a clear target, it'll spin its wheels on distraction. A mantra locks your attention on what matters.
- **Reinforces Identity:** The words you repeat become the stories you believe. When your mantra reflects who you're choosing to be ("I am a relentless learner," "I embrace every challenge"), it rewires your self-image.
- **Anchors Against Adversity:** Life will inevitably throw curveballs. Your mantra is a mental lifeline you can grab in moments of doubt or discouragement.

HOW TO CREATE YOUR MANTRA

1. **Identify Your Core Value or Promise**
    - Reflect on what you believe at a deep level. Is it faith? ("All things are possible through Him.")

Courage? ("Fear is fuel for my growth.") Contribution? ("I impact lives with every action.")
- Write down the one idea you'd like to carry through every decision, every conversation, and every setback.

2. **Choose Your Inspiration**
    - **Quote**: Maybe there's a line from Churchill, "Success is not final, failure is not fatal."
    - **Scripture**: Perhaps you're drawn to Proverbs 3:5: "Trust in the Lord with all your heart."
    - **Personal Creed**: Even a phrase you've spoken to yourself in the past can serve as a seed.

3. **Distill to a Short Phrase**
    - Aim for three to seven words max. Long sentences fade; compact rhythms anchor.
    - Strip away any extra words. For example:
        - Original: "I trust that God is guiding my path and providing everything I need."
        - Mantra: "God guides my path."

4. **Test It in the Trenches**
    - Speak it aloud as you brush your teeth.
    - Whisper it during your commute.
    - Feel the emotional shift: Does your energy rise? If it falls flat, iterate until you find a phrase that sparks conviction.

5. **Embed It into Ritual**
    - Write your mantra on a three-by-five card by your bedside.
    - Make it your smartphone lock screen.
    - Wake up each morning and repeat your mantra three times.
    - Start morning devotions or journaling by declaring it three times.

SAMPLE MANTRAS

Growth Mindset
- "Progress over perfection."
- "I learn, I adapt, I excel."

Abundance Mindset
- "Sources of good surround me."
- "I am a magnet for blessings."

Faith-Driven
- "With God, all things are possible."
- "I walk by faith, not by sight."

Courage and Action
- "Fortune favors the bold."
- "Do it afraid."

CREATE YOUR MANTRA

1. Grab a blank page and jot down three words that define who you're becoming.
2. Pair them with a scripture, quote, or conviction that resonates.
3. Carve it down to a one-liner you can carry in your heart and on your lips every day.

This simple commitment, a few seconds each morning, will compound over days, weeks, and months. Your mantra becomes the mental soundtrack of your Personal Success System. Speak it, believe it, and live it. Watch the mindset shift you need to quit jacking around and execute at your highest level.

Scan to Download the Personal Mantra Builder™ Tool:

Once you get your mindset right, you need to have clarity about who you are and what matters to you before you move forward in solidifying your vision and goals.

PRACTICAL APPLICATION IN BUILDING YOUR PERSONAL SUCCESS SYSTEM: MINDSET

Now it is time to take everything you've learned about mindset and develop your winning mindset by completing your Mindset Maximizer tool.

Scan To Download the Mindset Maximizer™ Tool

SECTION SUMMARY AND KEY TAKEAWAYS: MINDSET

Overview: Mindset is foundational to achieving personal growth and success. Goals often fail due to the lack of a growth mindset, a mindset that welcomes challenges and is resilient in the face of setbacks. The journey toward personal success begins with changing one's mindset, habits, and actions, as these shape one's current and future realities.

KEY TAKEAWAYS

1. **Mindset is Essential:**
    - Without a growth mindset, obstacles and inconveniences easily halt progress.
    - Mindset determines your ability to sustain growth and success.

2. **Four Principles of Personal Growth:**
    - **Self-Awareness:** Recognize strengths, weaknesses, and limiting beliefs.
    - **Ownership of Growth:** Take full responsibility for your own development.
    - **Action-Oriented:** Growth comes through taking concrete actions.
    - **Trusted Relationships:** Surround yourself with people who encourage and support your growth.

3. **Defining Success:**
   - Success aligns with personal fulfillment, continuous growth, meaningful goals, resilience, adaptability, and positive impact.

4. **Stop Making Excuses:**
   - Excuses help you justify in your mind, keeping the status quo. When you stop making excuses, you step out of your comfort zone and into your better future.

5. **Invest in Yourself**
   - Growth always requires investment of time, energy, and financial resources into the people, programs, and resources required to grow.

ACTION ITEMS

- ➤ Develop clarity about your current mindset: identify limiting beliefs and commit to a growth mindset.
- ➤ Engage in self-assessment to become more self-aware.
- ➤ Take responsibility for your growth by setting clear, actionable goals.
- ➤ Build relationships that encourage accountability and mutual growth.

ESTABLISHING A WINNING MINDSET

Overview: A winning mindset combines growth and abundance perspectives, overcomes limiting beliefs and cognitive biases, and cultivates resilience. Mindset shapes your interpretation of experiences and your capacity for success.

KEY TAKEAWAYS

1. **The GAIN Mindset Matrix™**
   - **Grow:** Embrace Challenges as Your Training Ground
   - **Adapt:** Persist Through Setbacks and Shift with Purpose
   - **Inspire:** Learn from the Wins of Others Without Comparison
   - **Navigate:** Believe in Unlimited Potential and Seek New Paths
   - Then – **Elevate**: Focus Outward Toward Contribution

2. **Removing Limiting Beliefs**
   - Limiting beliefs are often irrational and self-imposed barriers.
   - Replace negative beliefs with empowering thoughts through deliberate reframing.

3. **Winning the War of the Mind**
   - Develop mental resilience to remain focused and positive despite setbacks.
   - Adopt clarity of purpose and perseverance, learning from the resilience of individuals like Thomas Edison and J.K. Rowling.

4. **Create Your Personal Mantra**
    - Create a short, potent phrase or verse that captures your highest values and reminds you who you're becoming.

ACTION ITEMS

- ➤ Regularly challenge and reframe limiting beliefs through positive affirmations and visualization.
- ➤ Actively seek feedback, embrace risks, and continuously engage in learning opportunities.
- ➤ Practice mindfulness and gratitude to maintain emotional balance and positivity.
- ➤ Cultivate strong relationships and build a supportive network.
- ➤ Implement resilience-building practices like clear goal setting, mindfulness, self-compassion, and continuous personal growth.
- ➤ Repeat your mantra every morning (and whenever you need a mental reset) to prime your brain for growth, abundance, and intentional action.

CONCLUSION

Your mindset determines your potential for success and fulfillment. Adopting a growth and abundance mindset, overcoming cognitive biases, and fostering resilience create the foundation necessary to achieve meaningful, sustained success. By transforming your mindset, you lay the groundwork for lasting personal and professional growth.

PART 2

Stop chasing goals that aren't yours. Know your DNA.
Own your purpose. Build like you mean it.

D N A

DNA represents your core identity, values, and internal patterns. It shapes how you think, behave, and respond to life. When you refine your DNA, you shift the foundation of who you are, enabling transformation that creates lasting, meaningful change.

6

DISCOVERING YOUR DNA

UNCOVERING THE FOUNDATION OF YOUR SUCCESS

The journey toward success doesn't start with external actions; it begins with understanding who you are at your core, your values, purpose, and vision. Just as DNA serves as the blueprint for all living organisms, your DNA is the foundation for the life you want to create. It influences the decisions you make, the habits you build, and the goals you pursue.

Without clarity in this area, you may find yourself drifting aimlessly, achieving things that don't truly fulfill you, or worse, feeling stuck and disconnected from what really matters.

Your DNA is made up of two critical components.

1. **Your Purpose:** The reason you exist, the impact you are meant to make, and the driving force behind your actions.
2. **Your Values:** The guiding principles that shape your decisions, behaviors, and priorities.

CLARITY OF PURPOSE

Just as a pilot wouldn't take off without a flight plan, you shouldn't embark on a journey to success without first defining your internal compass. Clarity of purpose and values brings focus, confidence, and resilience, especially when challenges arise. When you know who you are and why you do what you do, you won't be easily swayed by distractions, setbacks, or the opinions of others. Instead, you'll make decisions with conviction and take action with unwavering commitment.

MY PURPOSE AND VALUES (DNA) / THE WHY

When I reflect on my health and weight loss journey that I shared in the introduction, one thing stands out: it wasn't just about losing weight. It was about purpose.

My *why* ran deeper than wanting to look or feel better. I realized that my health directly impacted my ability to lead, serve, and show up for the people who depend on me most—my family, my team, and my mission. When I connected my goals to that deeper purpose, everything changed.

What started as a physical goal became a personal mission. I wasn't driven by numbers on a scale but by the desire for energy, presence, and endurance to live out my calling. That clarity transformed my mindset and kept me anchored when motivation faded.

That's the power of knowing your DNA—your why. Purpose turns ordinary goals into commitments that endure.

What does purpose-driven success look like? We can examine the legendary tennis champion, Serena Williams, and her purpose-driven legacy of success.

A LEGACY OF PURPOSE-DRIVEN SUCCESS

Success isn't about collecting wins—it's about walking in purpose, tearing down the walls that hold you back, and becoming the kind of person who inspires others to do the same.

CLARITY OF PURPOSE: SERENA WILLIAMS DOMINATING TENNIS AND INSPIRING OTHERS

What does it actually look like to live with unshakable purpose and pursue goals that truly matter? How does someone turn clarity of vision into daily discipline, and eventually, a meaningful legacy? The story you're about to revisit isn't just a tribute to greatness; it's a practical illustration of how living on purpose produces extraordinary outcomes, both in personal achievement and in lasting impact.

Serena Williams offers us more than a highlight reel of championship wins. Her life and career model how purpose, values, and vision—when clearly defined and consistently acted upon—become the foundation for lasting success. As you reflect on her example, don't just admire it. Ask yourself: What does this mean for me? How can I take the same principles and begin applying them to the seven core areas of my life? Because the truth is, you don't need to be a tennis icon to build a legacy. You just need clarity, commitment, and a system that keeps you aligned. That's what this next section is here to help you build.

True success isn't just about winning; it's about breaking barriers, staying grounded in your values, and using your influence to empower others. That kind of success begins with knowing exactly why you're doing what you're doing.

CLARITY OF PURPOSE: THE POWER BEHIND SERENA'S DOMINATION

Serena Williams didn't become one of the greatest athletes of all time by chance or raw talent alone. Her success was intentional—rooted in a clearly defined purpose and mission that guided her every move. From an early age, her father, Richard Williams, instilled a vision: not just to play tennis, but to change tennis. The sport had long been dominated by wealthy, white players. Serena and her sister Venus entered that world with a greater mission—to break down barriers, change perceptions, and inspire others who looked like them.

That bigger *why* gave Serena her edge. Winning Grand Slam titles wasn't the ultimate goal; it was a byproduct of something deeper. Her purpose wasn't just personal; it was generational. She wanted to prove that with belief, work ethic, and resilience, any obstacle could be overcome. Research shows that individuals with a strong sense of purpose are more resilient, more focused, and better equipped to handle stress and adversity.[47]

VALUES IN ACTION: HOW SHE TURNED BELIEFS INTO BREAKTHROUGHS

Serena's core values weren't abstract ideas—they showed up in her daily actions. Consider these:

Discipline and Work Ethic:

Serena trained longer, harder, and more consistently than anyone else. Her fitness routine was brutal because she knew greatness required more than talent—it demanded preparation. This aligns with research on deliberate practice and mastery—where consistent effort over time predicts high-level performance.[48]

Resilience and Mental Toughness:

From public criticism to personal health scares, Serena never let external pressure define her. She faced racism, sexism, and skepticism, yet kept showing up stronger every time. Studies confirm that resilience is often enhanced when one's actions align with core values and a sense of higher meaning.[49]

Confidence and Self-Belief:

Serena didn't wait for the world to validate her. She operated with the belief that she was made for greatness—and that mindset fueled her ability to perform under pressure. Psychologists call this "self-efficacy," and it's a critical factor in goal achievement.[50]

Empowerment and Legacy:

Off the court, she became a force for justice, equity, and opportunity. She used her voice and resources to champion causes bigger than herself, especially for women and people of color.

BEYOND THE COURT: A PURPOSE THAT MULTIPLIED

Serena didn't stop at tennis. She became a successful entrepreneur, investor, philanthropist, and advocate. Her impact expanded far beyond her profession—because her identity wasn't tied to just one role. It was tied to her purpose.

When you know your *why*, it follows you into every area of life. That's the kind of clarity that multiplies.

She used her platform to launch businesses, fund underrepresented founders, support young athletes, and speak up for justice. That's what purpose does; it scales. And it's exactly what this book is designed to help you do.

NOW, APPLY IT TO YOU: START WITH YOUR DNA

This isn't just Serena's story. It's a call for you to clarify your own.

Know Your Purpose and Values:
These form your internal compass—fuel for your resilience and the filter for your decisions.

Define Your Purpose and Values:
Identify what truly matters to you. Purpose creates intrinsic motivation, the kind that lasts long after the hype fades.[51]

Clarify Purpose Across All Areas of Life:
Success isn't one-dimensional. The seven core areas—Faith, Fitness, Family, Focus (Work), Finances, Friends, and Fun—are where your purpose comes to life.

This isn't about vague self-reflection. It's about building a Personal Success System based on who you are and what you were made to do. When you discover your DNA—your unique design, natural strengths, and aligned values—you gain clarity. And with clarity comes direction, focus, and power.

Let's start building that system.

THE SCIENCE BEHIND PURPOSE AND GOAL ACHIEVEMENT

Purpose isn't just a feel-good concept; it's a proven driver of performance and well-being. When you understand your why, you engage more deeply, recover faster from setbacks, and sustain progress over the long term. Research on *self-concordant goals*—those aligned with personal values and identity—shows that they foster higher persistence, greater resilience, and enhanced well-being compared to externally driven goals.[52][53]

Purpose transforms challenges from energy-draining obstacles into fuel for persistence. It sharpens focus, filters out distractions, and frames adversity as part of the journey rather than a deviation. Without it, you risk pursuing goals shaped by societal pressure, family expectations, or social media trends—only to find you've been climbing the wrong ladder all along.

WHY PURPOSE IS THE FIRST STEP IN THE PERSONAL SUCCESS SYSTEM

In the Personal Success System, after you set your winning mindset, you next must get clear about your DNA—your design, your purpose, your why—because goal achievement without purpose alignment often leads to burnout or dissatisfaction. Purpose discovery isn't a one-time event; it's a continual refinement process ensuring that your goals remain tethered to your deepest values.

When goals are purpose-aligned, research shows they generate stronger intrinsic motivation, increased persistence, and more consistent follow-through.[54][55] In a meta-analysis of over 100 goal-setting studies, alignment between personal values and goals was a key predictor of goal success rates.[56]

1. Clarity of Purpose Amplifies Motivation

Purpose is one of the strongest predictors of follow-through. In a longitudinal study, people with a well-defined sense of purpose were more likely to sustain effort on challenging tasks and less likely to give up under stress.[57] This is because purpose fuels intrinsic motivation—the kind of drive that persists even when external rewards fade.

- **Why this matters:** Intrinsic motivation links to higher creativity, problem-solving ability, and persistence in adversity.[58]
- **Application:** Revisit your why regularly to keep your emotional connection to your goals strong.

2. Purpose-Aligned Goals Have Higher Success Rates

Goals rooted in personal meaning avoid the quiet self-destruction common to "should" goals—those set from obligation, fear, or comparison. Research in the *Journal of Personality and Social Psychology* found that people pursuing self-concordant goals were more likely to take sustained action and experience increased satisfaction after goal attainment.[59]

- **Statistically significant difference:** In applied settings, purpose-aligned goals are often completed at nearly double the rate of misaligned goals.[60]
- **Application:** Before committing to a goal, ask, "Does this reflect who I am and what I value?"

3. Purpose Enhances Focus and Prioritization

A clear sense of purpose acts as a filter for decision-making. In one study, participants with higher purpose scores were better able to prioritize long-term objectives over short-term temptations, demonstrating greater self-regulation.[61]

- **Why this matters:** Decision fatigue and distraction are major causes of failed goals. Purpose reduces both by providing a guiding framework for what gets your time and energy.
- **Application:** Use the question, "Does this move me toward my purpose or away from it?" to shape your daily calendar.

4. Purpose Elevates Teams

Purpose isn't only a personal advantage; it's a collective performance multiplier. Gallup's *State of the Global Workplace* report shows that teams with a shared purpose are more engaged, more collaborative, and up to 70 percent more likely to meet performance goals.[62]

- **Why this matters:** In organizations, shared purpose builds trust, psychological safety, and alignment—critical components of high performance.
- **Application:** For team leaders, clearly articulate and regularly reinforce the team's collective "why."

5. Purpose Has Long-Term Impact

Purpose predicts not just short-term achievement but also major life outcomes. A 14-year longitudinal study found that individuals with a higher sense of purpose had better health and lower mortality risk and were more likely to achieve significant life milestones.[63]

- **Why this matters:** Purpose acts as a stabilizing force, helping people maintain consistent progress even as circumstances change.
- **Application:** View purpose as a lifelong compass, not a single-destination map.

WHY PURPOSE WORKS: THE PSYCHOLOGY BEHIND IT

Purpose is powerful because it changes both your mental framework and your emotional engagement:

- **Resilience:** Purpose helps reframe setbacks as part of a meaningful narrative, encouraging perseverance.[64]
- **Engagement:** People with strong purpose report higher daily energy and engagement levels.[65]
- **Mental Health:** Purpose reduces stress, anxiety, and burnout, creating psychological conditions that support sustained achievement.[66]

THIS IS WHY WE START WITH DNA

Without a clearly defined purpose, any system you build will be fragile. With it, you gain clarity, drive, resilience, and meaningful results. Purpose is not static; it should be cultivated, refined, and revisited regularly. When your goals align with your DNA, achievement becomes inevitable and deeply satisfying.

THIS IS WHY WE GET CLEAR WITH DNA

With the Personal Success System, you learn to start by uncovering your DNA: your **design**, your **values**, and your **purpose**—your why. Without this foundation, any system you build will be fragile because you'll be operating without a clear compass for decision-making. With it, you gain clarity, drive, resilience, and results that align with your true identity.

Values act as the guardrails for your life. They define what is non-negotiable, guide how you treat others, and influence which opportunities you accept or reject. When your goals align with both your purpose and your values, you not only know where you're going but also ensure you're taking the right road to get there.

Purpose is the directional force—your reason for getting up in the morning—while values are the principles that determine how you travel that road. Together, they create a personal success filter that helps you make faster, more confident decisions, reduces regret, and keeps you anchored when circumstances shift.

7

DEFINING YOUR PURPOSE WITH GRIT

Integrating purpose into your goal-setting process is essential for ensuring that every step you take moves you toward a life of meaning and success.

1. DEFINE YOUR PURPOSE

Your purpose is your *why*, the reason you do what you do. Without a well-defined purpose, goals can feel arbitrary or uninspiring. The first step to harnessing purpose for goal achievement is to clarify your personal mission. In the PSS, we use the GRIT Method™ to help you develop and define your mission statement.

THE GRIT METHOD: A QJA SYSTEM FOR CRAFTING YOUR PERSONAL PURPOSE STATEMENT

Your personal mission statement is more than just words on a page—it's your internal compass. An internal compass to help you show up intentionally, make decisions with confidence, and stay grounded in what matters most.

In the Quit Jacking Around (QJA) Personal Success System, we use the GRIT Method to help you uncover and articulate your purpose with clarity and strength. Each letter represents a key step in discovering a Purpose Statement that's real, relevant, and resolute.

G — Grind: What work are you willing to do even when it's hard?

"What am I willing to struggle for?"

Purpose isn't about what excites you in theory; it's what you're willing to commit to in practice. The "grind" represents your capacity for meaningful effort, not meaningless hustle.

Ask yourself:

- ➢ What challenges am I willing to face over and over again?
- ➢ What would I keep doing even if I didn't get recognition or quick rewards?
- ➢ What mission would still matter to me when things get hard?

Write it down.

"I'm willing to grind for ___ because ___."

R — Resonance: What makes your soul say yes?

"What feels deeply fulfilling?"

This is your emotional alignment: the work, causes, or outcomes that stir something within you. You don't have to be good at it yet. You just have to care.

Ask yourself:

> - What activities, people, or causes light me up?
> - What wrongs do I feel called to right?
> - What brings me joy, flow, or a sense of peace?

Write it down.

> "I feel resonance when I ___ because it helps me ___."

I — Impact: Who do you want to serve, and how?

"What change do I want to create in the world?"

Purpose is almost always relational; it involves making a difference outside yourself. It's not just about what you want, but what you want for others.

Ask yourself:

> - Who benefits when I'm at my best?
> - What ripple effect do I want my life to have?
> - What problems do I feel equipped—or called—to solve?

Write it down.

> "The impact I want to create is ___ in the lives of ___."

T — Trajectory: Where is this all leading?

"What legacy do I want to leave?"

Trajectory is about your long view. What kind of story do you want your life to tell? It helps you zoom out, clarify your vision, and stay on course.

Ask yourself:

- What do I want to be remembered for?
- What unfinished business burns in my gut?
- If I could be known for one thing, what would it be?

Write it down.

"The legacy I want to leave is ___ by living a life of ___."

BRINGING IT ALL TOGETHER

Now, it's your turn. Create your own GRIT statement by reflecting on each step.

- What am I willing to Grind for?
- What deeply Resonates with me?
- What Impact do I want to create?
- What Trajectory am I aiming toward?

Combine your answers into a GRIT-inspired Purpose Statement using this customizable structure and write your GRIT Purpose Statement. Don't aim for perfection; aim for truth. You can refine it over time, but getting something on paper gives you clarity and power.

"My purpose is to *[grind for what matters]* with *[resonance from what fulfills me]*, to create *[impact]* in the lives of *[who you serve]*, and to build a legacy of *[trajectory]*."

Example: "My purpose is to fight for strong families with the fulfillment I find in helping men lead with love and clarity, to create emotional health and connection in the lives of overwhelmed dads, and to build a legacy of generational transformation."

> Use these steps as a guideline for creating your GRIT statement.
>
> 1. Set aside 30–60 minutes.
> 2. Journal your responses for each GRIT step.
> 3. Draft your first version of your GRIT Purpose Statement.
> 4. Say it aloud. Share it with someone. Revisit it weekly.

1. Set aside 30–60 minutes.

Purpose work requires space—both mental and physical. Block out uninterrupted time in a quiet place where you can think clearly and reflect deeply. Turn off distractions, silence your phone, and give yourself permission to slow down. This isn't busywork; it's soul work. You're taking a step toward defining who you are, why you do what you do, and where you're going. Treat it like a meeting with your future self—the version of you who's living with clarity and conviction.

2. Journal your responses for each GRIT step.

As you move through each part of the GRIT framework, write freely. Don't edit yourself or try to sound impressive—just be honest. The goal is depth, not polish. Let your thoughts, memories, and emotions flow onto the page. Sometimes clarity comes in fragments, stories, or even sentences that surprise you. The more authentic your reflections, the more powerful your purpose statement will become. This is where you connect your "why" to your lived experiences.

3. Draft your first version of your GRIT Purpose Statement.

Now, bring it all together. Using what you've uncovered in your journaling, craft your first version of a GRIT Purpose Statement—a clear, concise declaration that captures what drives you, what fulfills you, the impact you want to make, and the legacy you're building. Don't worry about making it perfect. Purpose evolves over time. What matters most is that it feels real, energizing, and aligned with who you are today. This is your starting point, your compass.

4. Say it aloud. Share it with someone. Revisit it weekly.

Purpose gains power when it's spoken and shared. Saying your GRIT Statement aloud activates belief and accountability—it moves it from an idea in your head to a conviction in your heart. Share it with someone you trust—a spouse, friend, mentor, or coach—and invite feedback. Then, make it a living document. Revisit it weekly to refine, reflect, and realign. As you grow, your clarity will deepen, and your statement will sharpen into something that truly anchors your actions and decisions.

Scan to Download the GRIT Framework™ Tool

2. ALIGN GOALS WITH YOUR PURPOSE

Purpose-driven goals hold transformative power because they connect what you *do* to who you *are* and *why* you do it. When your goals are rooted in purpose, they move beyond surface-level achievements and become expressions of your deeper values, beliefs, and vision for life. This alignment creates a powerful internal drive—one that keeps you moving forward even when challenges arise or motivation fades.

Instead of chasing goals for external validation or fleeting rewards, purpose-driven goals tap into intrinsic motivation—the kind that fuels consistency, passion, and resilience. You're not just checking boxes; you're advancing something that matters to you at a soul level. This clarity brings focus, helping you prioritize what truly deserves your time and energy while eliminating distractions that don't align with your mission.

When you align your goals with your purpose and values, your decisions become easier, your actions become more intentional, and your progress becomes more fulfilling. You begin to measure success not just by outcomes, but by the integrity of your journey—by whether your goals reflect who you were created to be and the impact you're called to make.

In short, purpose gives your goals *meaning*, meaning gives your effort *momentum*, and momentum produces *lasting results*. The deeper your alignment, the greater your sense of fulfillment—because you're not just achieving goals, you're living your purpose.

STEPS TO ALIGN GOALS WITH PURPOSE

1. Break down long-term aspirations into smaller, purpose-aligned goals.
    - Example: If your purpose is to "empower others through education," set specific goals like hosting workshops, writing a book, or mentoring.

2. Ask yourself:
    - Does this goal align with my core values and purpose?
    - How does achieving this goal help fulfill my deeper mission?
    - What impact will this goal have on me and others?

> 3. Filter out non-purpose-driven goals.
>   - Avoid setting goals just because they sound impressive; focus on what truly matters to you.

3. MAINTAIN PURPOSE IN THE FACE OF ADVERSITY

Challenges are inevitable, but staying grounded in your *why* will help you push through obstacles. When difficulties arise—and they always do—your purpose acts as an anchor, keeping you steady when everything around you feels uncertain. Without a clear sense of why you're doing what you're doing, even small setbacks can feel overwhelming and discouraging. But when your actions are rooted in a deep and meaningful reason, challenges become opportunities to prove your commitment, strengthen your character, and clarify your direction.

Your *why* gives pain a purpose. It transforms struggle from something to avoid into something that refines and strengthens you. Every obstacle becomes a test of alignment—a question of whether you truly believe in what you're pursuing. When your motivation comes from something bigger than comfort or convenience, you'll find the endurance to persevere long after others have quit.

Think of your *why* as a compass in the storm. External circumstances may shift, plans may fail, and people may doubt you, but your *why* reminds you of who you are and what truly matters. It's not just about surviving challenges; it's about using them as fuel for growth. Staying connected to your deeper purpose allows you to adapt, learn, and come back stronger.

In practical terms, this means taking time to revisit your *why* regularly. Write it down. Speak it out loud. Reflect on it when frustration sets in. Ask yourself: *Why did I start? Who am I doing this for? What would it mean if I quit now?* These questions reconnect you to your mission and reignite your motivation. Over time, you'll begin to see challenges not as detours, but as essential parts of the journey that prepare you for greater success.

STRATEGIES FOR STAYING PURPOSE-DRIVEN DURING TOUGH TIMES

- ➢ Revisit your Purpose Statement. Keep it visible in your workspace.
- ➢ Remind yourself why your goal matters. Journaling about the bigger impact can reignite motivation.
- ➢ Stay flexible. If circumstances change, adapt your approach while staying true to your mission.

TOOLS TO REINFORCE PURPOSE

1. Journaling
    - Daily reflection prompts:
        - ○ *"What did I do today that moved me closer to fulfilling my purpose?"*
        - ○ *"What challenges did I face, and how did I respond with purpose?"*

2. Mind Mapping
    - Create a visual representation of how your goals connect to your bigger mission.

3. Vision Board
    - Display images, quotes, and symbols representing your purpose-driven goals.

4. Digital Tools
    - Use apps like Notion, MindMeister, or Habitica to organize and track purpose-driven goals.

Example: Purpose-Driven Goal Framework

Component	Example
Purpose	To improve community health and well-being
Long-Term Goal	Establish a local wellness center
Short-Term Goals	Research funding opportunities Build partnerships with health providers Host community wellness workshops
Action Plan	Break each short-term goal into actionable steps

FINAL THOUGHT: INTEGRATING PURPOSE INTO YOUR DAILY LIFE

Purpose isn't just about setting a mission; it's about **living it daily.** When you align your goals with purpose, you transform success from a mere destination into a fulfilling journey.

> **YOUR NEXT STEP**
>
> 1. Write your Purpose Statement.
> 2. Define at least three purpose-driven goals.
> 3. Take the first small step toward those goals today.

Your purpose is your greatest asset. Harness it, and success will follow. Once you are clear on your purpose, the next step is to gain clarity on your personal values.

After completing this section, update your Vision Execution Snapshot so it reflects what you just clarified and stays current and aligned.

8

DISCOVER YOUR DNA—STEP 2: GAIN CLARITY ON YOUR PERSONAL VALUES

Your values are the cornerstones of your decision-making and success. They define what truly matters to you and serve as a guiding force for your personal and professional life. Without clearly defined values, it's easy to get distracted by external pressures, pursue goals that don't fulfill you, or feel lost in decision-making.

Here are five strategies to identify your core values. Once you have identified your core values, you can align them with your goals to achieve clarity of direction, increased motivation, and fulfillment.

1: REFLECTIVE QUESTIONS TO IDENTIFY VALUES

Before you can integrate your values into your life, you need to clarify what they are. These powerful reflection questions will help you uncover the themes that define who you are and what you stand for. Consider these four questions and write down your responses.

1. **What qualities or principles do I admire in others?**
   - Think about the people you respect the most.
   - What values make them admirable?

   Example Values: Integrity, kindness, perseverance, and leadership.

   Real-World Example: If you admire people who always keep their word, then integrity is likely a core value for you.

2. **When am I happiest or most fulfilled?**
   - Recall moments when you felt deep joy and purpose.
   - What activities, environments, or relationships were involved?

   Example Values: Creativity, connection, adventure, personal growth, and service.

   Real-World Example: If you feel most alive when helping others, then service or compassion may be among your top values.

3. **What situations make me uncomfortable or upset?**
   - Identify what bothers you to help clarify your non-negotiables.
   - What behaviors or circumstances feel out of alignment with your values?

   Example Values: Justice, honesty, respect, and inclusivity.

Real-World Example: If dishonesty in the workplace frustrates you, then integrity and transparency are likely key values for you.

4. **What legacy would I like to leave behind?**
   - Visualize how you want to be remembered.
   - What impact do you want to make?

Example Values: Impact, generosity, wisdom, leadership, and innovation.

2: VALUE CATEGORIES AND PRACTICAL EXAMPLES

In the table below, review the Value Categories to see which ones speak to you the most. Then reflect on the example core values for each category and make a list of which core values feel like the right fit for your life. Try identifying 5–10 core values to begin. The Real-World Applications for these values can inspire you as you look to establish goals based on your values later in the book.

Value Category	Core Values	Real-World Application
Personal Growth	Curiosity, Learning, Self-Improvement	Read personal development books, take courses, and seek mentorship.
Connection and Relationships	Family, Friendship, Empathy	Schedule quality time with loved ones, actively listen, and prioritize deep relationships.

Integrity	Honesty, Trustworthiness, Accountability	Keep promises, be transparent, admit mistakes, and take responsibility.
Service to Others	Generosity, Compassion, Community	Volunteer, mentor, and donate time and resources to causes you care about.
Creativity	Innovation, Originality, Expression	Write, paint, design, or find creative solutions in work and life.
Resilience	Perseverance, Adaptability, Grit	Develop mindfulness, exercise regularly, and push through adversity.
Justice and Equality	Fairness, Advocacy, Inclusivity	Support social causes and stand up against discrimination.
Freedom and Independence	Autonomy, Self-Sufficiency, Empowerment	Start a business, travel solo, and make financial decisions that increase independence.
Health and Well-Being	Physical, Mental, Emotional Health	Prioritize exercise, seek therapy, and practice self-care.

3: LIST AND PRIORITIZE YOUR TOP FIVE CORE VALUES

Once you've reviewed the value categories and identified your top core values, it's time to narrow them down to the five most essential values that define you.

HOW TO PRIORITIZE YOUR VALUES

1. Identify which values resonate with you most.
2. Rank them based on importance.
3. Ensure they reflect your authentic self, not external influences.

Example:

1. Service – Helping others brings me the greatest fulfillment.
2. Integrity – I believe in being honest and transparent in all situations.
3. Growth – Continuous learning is a priority for me.
4. Resilience – I want to overcome challenges and become stronger.
5. Connection – Relationships with loved ones are my foundation.

HOW THIS STEP IMPACTS YOUR LIFE

Career Decisions: If integrity is a top value, you'll seek roles in ethical organizations.

Relationships: If connection is a key value, you'll prioritize time with family and friends.

Personal Development: If growth is a value, you'll commit to lifelong learning.

Once you've identified your top five values, you can add them to the Vision-Execution Snapshot Tool discussed earlier in the book.

FINAL THOUGHT: LIVING IN ALIGNMENT WITH YOUR VALUES

Your values are not just words on a page; they are the foundation of your daily actions, decisions, and goals.

When you live in alignment with your values and purpose, you feel more fulfilled and energized.

Decision-making becomes simpler and more intentional. You experience greater clarity, confidence, and impact.

YOUR NEXT STEPS

1. Identify your top five values and write them down.
2. Share them with someone for feedback and refine as needed.
3. Add your purpose and values to the Vision-Execution Snapshot.
4. Apply your values to your daily life, work, and goals.

By taking these steps, you will have a solid foundation for purpose-driven success—one that ensures every action you take leads to deeper fulfillment and a lasting legacy.

Scan to Download the Values Solidifier™ Tool

THE POWER OF UNDERSTANDING YOUR DNA (PURPOSE + VALUES) IN ACHIEVING YOUR GOALS

Success isn't just about setting and achieving goals; it's about setting the right goals that align with your purpose and values. When you take the time to define your personal DNA—your core purpose, values, and vision—you create a foundation for intentional, meaningful success.

Without this clarity, you risk chasing goals that don't truly fulfill you, leaving you feeling unfulfilled even after achieving them.

By understanding your why (purpose) and how (values), you ensure that every goal you set moves you toward the life you truly want to create. Purpose-driven, values-aligned goals keep you motivated, resilient in the face of challenges, and deeply fulfilled in your accomplishments.

As you move forward, use your Purpose Statement and core values as a guide, filtering every decision, action, and goal through them. When you align your ambitions with your true self, success becomes more than an achievement; it becomes a life of impact, fulfillment, and lasting significance.

Once you have gained clarity on your purpose and values, you can start to build the vision picture you want to move toward. The next section will give you the direction to make this happen.

DISCOVERING YOUR DNA SUMMARY

By diligently following these steps and regularly revisiting your DNA (Purpose + Values)™, you'll establish a strong foundation for lasting and meaningful success.

KEY TAKEAWAYS

Foundation of Success: Your success journey must start by clearly understanding your personal "DNA"—your purpose and core values. Without this, achievements may feel unfulfilling or misaligned.

Purpose: The deep, intrinsic reason behind your actions, your impact, and the driving motivation for your goals.

Values: Your fundamental principles that shape decisions, actions, and priorities.

Importance of Clarity: Clearly defined purpose and values provide resilience, motivation, and direction, helping navigate challenges effectively.

- Real-Life Examples: My personal health journey (motivated by family and well-being) and Serena Williams (driven by breaking barriers and inspiring others) highlight the power of purpose and values.
- Scientific Backing: Research consistently shows that a clear purpose significantly boosts goal achievement, resilience, life satisfaction, and overall success.

ACTION ITEMS

→ **Define Your Purpose** with the GRIT Framework
→ Reflect deeply on what energizes you, the impact you wish to make, your strengths, and your desired legacy.
→ Craft a clear personal Purpose Statement using this structure: *My purpose is to [grind for what matters] with [resonance from what fulfills me], to create [impact] in the lives of [who you serve], and to build a legacy of [trajectory].*
→ **Clarify Your Values:** Identify your top five core values by reflecting on admired qualities, moments of fulfillment, discomfort triggers, and desired legacy.

Prioritize these values and integrate them into your Purpose Statement

→ Align goals with DNA.
  - Evaluate your goals and ensure alignment with your purpose and values.
→ Break down long-term aspirations into meaningful short-term objectives.
→ Maintain purpose during adversity.
  - Keep your Purpose Statement and top five values visible and revisit them regularly, especially during challenging times.

TOOLS TO REINFORCE YOUR DNA

1. **Journaling:** Reflect daily on your actions related to your purpose and values, and on the challenges you face.

2. **Mind Mapping:** Visually link a goal to your broader purpose.
3. **Vision Boards:** Create visual representations of your purpose-driven, values-based aspirations.
4. **Digital Tools:** Utilize apps like Notion and MindMeister to organize and track your purpose-driven journey.

After completing this section, update your Vision Execution Snapshot so it reflects what you just clarified and stays current and aligned.

PART 3

VISION

PERSONAL SUCCESS SYSTEM

Vision gives your life direction and meaning. It allows you to look beyond your current circumstances and define the future you want to create. A strong vision keeps you focused, aligned, and motivated as you work toward long-term growth and fulfillment.

9

CRAFTING YOUR VISION FOR THE FUTURE

Stop wandering aimlessly through life—craft your vision, chunk it down, and start turning your dreams into action. It's time to quit jacking around!

THE POWER OF KNOWING WHERE YOU'RE GOING

If you leave on a trip without knowing your desired destination, you'll never know where you'll end up. You might wander aimlessly, taking detours, making stops that don't serve your ultimate purpose, and possibly even ending up somewhere completely different from where you intended—if you even had an intention to begin with.

On the other hand, if you want to arrive at a specific destination, you need clarity about where that is and when you plan to get there. This knowledge helps you determine what actions you need to take right now to ensure you stay on course. Just as a pilot follows a flight plan or a captain steers a ship with a navigational chart, your life needs a clear vision to guide your journey. Without it, you risk drifting through life, reacting instead of proactively shaping your future.

Creating a vision is not about wishful thinking; it's about defining a tangible and compelling future that serves as a North Star for your decisions and actions. When you intentionally set a long-term vision for your life, you create a framework that informs every choice you make, from the habits you build to the opportunities you pursue. Your vision becomes a filter that helps you distinguish between distractions and priorities.

A long-term vision, however, isn't achieved all at once. It requires short-term vision pictures—clear, incremental goals that serve as steps along the journey. Think of these as checkpoints along your route, allowing you to measure progress, recalibrate when needed, and maintain motivation. Without these stepping stones, even the clearest vision can seem too distant and overwhelming, causing stagnation or doubt.

Looking back at my health and weight loss journey outlined in the introduction to this book, I needed to go beyond the general goal of "losing weight" and define exactly what *being healthy* would look like for me. I had to develop a clear vision of what the desired outcome would be for my health. That meant sitting down and identifying specific targets:

- How much weight did I need to lose?
- What should my body mass index (BMI) be?
- What key health markers, such as blood pressure, cholesterol, and other biomarkers, did I need to improve?

Weight loss is just one indicator of health, but my goal was more than just shedding pounds; I wanted true, sustainable well-being.

To ensure I was setting the right targets, I consulted with my doctor and a nutritionist, gathering expert insights on what a healthy version of *me* should look like. With their guidance, I mapped out my ideal weight, body composition, and overall health metrics.

But my vision wasn't just about numbers. I took time to visualize how I would *feel* once I reached my goal—how much more energy I'd have, how differently my body would move, and even what size clothing I would wear. The clearer I became about my desired outcome, the more motivated I was to take action.

MICHAEL PHELPS: THE POWER OF VISION AND MENTAL CLARITY IN ACHIEVING OLYMPIC GREATNESS

Michael Phelps, the most decorated Olympian of all time with 23 gold medals, is a perfect example of someone who used the power of vision to achieve extraordinary success. His dominance in swimming wasn't just a result of talent or hard work; it was also a direct outcome of mental clarity, goal setting, and visualization techniques.[67]

DEFINING THE VISION

From a young age, Phelps envisioned himself as the greatest swimmer in history. He worked with his coach, Bob Bowman, to set long-term goals, including winning multiple Olympic medals and breaking world records. Instead of merely wishing for success, he had a crystal-clear vision of what he wanted to achieve, down to the exact races he would dominate.[68]

VISUALIZATION: SEEING SUCCESS BEFORE IT HAPPENS

One of Phelps' most powerful tools was mental imagery. Every night before bed, he would close his eyes and visualize his races in meticulous detail—how he would push off the wall, every stroke he'd take, and even the moment he would touch the wall to finish. He didn't just imagine winning; he saw himself handling challenges, like a bad start or goggles filling with water.[69]

This mental clarity paid off in the 2008 Beijing Olympics during the 200-meter butterfly final. His goggles were completely filled with water early in the race, but instead of panicking, he relied on his mental vision and preparation. Since he had mentally rehearsed swimming blindfolded in training, he knew exactly how many strokes it took to reach the wall. He won the race and set a world record—all without being able to see.[70]

BREAKING GOALS INTO MILESTONES

Phelps didn't focus solely on Olympic gold. He and his coach chunked his vision into actionable goals:

- **Long-term goal:** Become the greatest swimmer of all time.
- **Three-year plan:** Dominate each Olympic cycle.
- **Yearly goals:** Break specific records and refine techniques.

- **Daily discipline:** Swim fifty miles per week, maintain a strict diet, and fine-tune his mindset.[71]

Each practice, every drill, and even his diet were aligned with his overarching vision.

THE LEGACY OF A VISION-DRIVEN LIFE

Phelps's career demonstrates that a clear vision fuels discipline, resilience, and long-term success. His ability to visualize, set specific goals, and stay focused through adversity helped him achieve a level of greatness no other Olympian has reached. Whether in sports, business, or personal growth, the power of vision transforms dreams into reality, just as it did for Michael Phelps.[72]

VISION: THE BLUEPRINT FOR A LIFE THAT MATTERS

If purpose is the engine that drives your life, then vision is the roadmap. A compelling vision gives direction to your purpose, translating your *why* into a picture of *what's next*.

Without vision, effort becomes scattered. With it, every step is intentional.

Psychological and business research consistently confirms that a clear, well-articulated vision dramatically increases the likelihood of achieving meaningful outcomes—in work, relationships, health, and life as a whole. Vision doesn't just inspire; it informs and organizes your goals into actionable progress.

1. CLEAR VISION ELEVATES GOAL ACHIEVEMENT

> It's one thing to want change; it's another to define it clearly.

A landmark study by Dr. Gail Matthews at Dominican University of California found that individuals are forty-two percent more likely to achieve their goals when they **write them down**.[73] That's because articulating a vision shifts a desire into a commitment; it engages both the rational and emotional centers of the brain.

Further research shows that individuals with specific, **well-defined goals** outperform those with vague aspirations by 20–25 percent.[74] Clarity is power, and in goal setting, it becomes a multiplier of results.

When your vision is clear, your focus sharpens, your motivation deepens, and the path to achievement transforms from possibility into purpose-driven progress.

2. VISUALIZATION ACTIVATES THE BRAIN'S SUCCESS CENTERS

> Vision setting isn't just philosophical; it's neurological.

Neuroscience studies reveal that when people visualize a vivid and compelling future, they activate the brain's prefrontal cortex, the region responsible for motivation, focus, decision-making, and strategic thinking.[75] In other words, having a clear vision literally primes your brain to solve problems and stay on course.

Even outside traditional goal-setting, visualization has proven effective. Athletes who practice mental imagery techniques see 10–15 percent improvements in performance, proving that the mind rehearses success before the body executes it.

Imagine what that kind of edge can mean in your personal or professional life.

3. VISION BOOSTS LEADERSHIP AND ORGANIZATIONAL PERFORMANCE

> A clear and compelling vision doesn't just inspire individuals—it measurably improves leadership effectiveness and organizational outcomes.

Research on transformational leadership shows that leaders who articulate and reinforce a shared vision significantly increase organizational commitment, which in turn drives higher levels of employee performance and team effectiveness.[76] Shared vision acts as a unifying force, aligning individual goals with collective objectives and strengthening engagement across teams.

In business, vision is not a slogan on the wall; it is a cultural catalyst that shapes behavior, commitment, and results.

4. LIFE VISION FUELS FULFILLMENT AND RESILIENCE

> When life gets hard, and it always does, a clear vision keeps you moving.

Studies on personal well-being show that people with a clearly defined life vision report up to 30 percent higher levels of happiness and satisfaction than those without direction.[77] They're also more resilient, navigating setbacks with perspective because they see each challenge as part of a larger story.

Vision doesn't eliminate obstacles; it makes them meaningful.

5. STRUCTURED VISION ACCELERATES SUCCESS

Having a vision is one thing; structuring it is another.

Research on goal frameworks shows that individuals who follow **SMART goals (Specific, Measurable, Achievable, Relevant, Time-Bound)**, which help crystallize vision into manageable steps, achieve their goals 76 percent of the time, compared to just 43 percent for those who don't use structured methods.[78]

Vision isn't just dreaming big. It's dreaming *clearly*, then organizing that dream into a system.

In the Quit Jacking Around Personal Success System, vision is the pivotal next step after uncovering your DNA (Purpose + Values). Once you know who you are and what you're meant to do, vision helps you paint a detailed picture of your future so your goals are not just random targets, but intentional milestones.

Purpose tells you *why*. Vision shows you *where*. When those two are clear, the *how* becomes much easier to figure out.

YOUR VISION IS YOUR FOUNDATION

A clear vision acts as the foundation of your success system. It fuels your motivation, aligns your actions, and provides a sense of purpose. Without it, you're left to react to life's circumstances rather than proactively shaping your own future. Whether you aim for personal growth, career success, financial freedom, or a lasting legacy, a well-defined vision gives you the roadmap to turn aspirations into reality.

THE POWER OF THINKING BIG

One of the greatest obstacles to growth isn't a lack of opportunity or talent; it's the limitations we place on our own vision. Often, people anchor their dreams to what they believe is realistic, shrinking their potential to the size of their current circumstances or past experiences. The truth is, history's greatest achievements, innovations, and personal transformations began with someone daring to imagine something much bigger than what seemed possible at the time.

BIG THINKING IS THE FUEL OF BIG RESULTS

When you allow yourself to think beyond your present reality, to envision goals that are ten times larger than your current situation, or to pursue what author Jim Collins calls Big Hairy Audacious Goals (BHAGs), you unlock new levels of creativity, energy, and resourcefulness within yourself.[79] Suddenly, you're not just solving for incremental improvement; you're expanding your entire field of possibilities. Even if you don't hit the exact target you set, the act of reaching for something bold inevitably leads to greater progress than playing it safe ever could.

VISION ALONE ISN'T ENOUGH

The magic happens when you combine big, inspiring goals with disciplined daily and weekly execution, the very heart of the Personal Success System. Every day that you act on your vision, no matter how small the step, you're compounding your growth. It's a principle seen in investing: small, consistent deposits grow exponentially over time. The same is true for your life, career, and relationships. Regularly taking action on your biggest vision, no matter how audacious, transforms impossible dreams into everyday reality, one deliberate step at a time.

AS YOU BUILD YOUR VISION-EXECUTION SNAPSHOT, DON'T HOLD BACK

Allow yourself to imagine a future that excites and even scares you a little.

- Write down a vision that stretches your comfort zone and invites you to become the person capable of achieving it.
    - Then, trust the process; show up, execute, and watch as your growth compounds into success far beyond what you can comprehend today.

The only true limits are those you set in your mind; set your sights higher, and your actions will follow.

THE LIFETIME VISUALIZER: DEFINING YOUR LEGACY

One of the most powerful ways to help craft your vision is by developing clarity, engaging in the **Lifetime Visualizer**™. This exercise forces you to think about your legacy, what truly matters, and the life you want to be remembered. Imagine you're writing your own eulogy for your closest friends and family to read as they are celebrating your life. What do you want them to say about you? What kind of impact have you made? What kind of person were you?

Consider the core areas of your life as you consider your eulogy as if you had fulfilled all your dreams and goals. Be specific; describe your accomplishments, the lives you've touched, and the values you lived. This exercise provides clarity on what truly matters to you and serves as a foundation for building a meaningful vision for your future. Use The 7 Fs Matrix ™ in the PSS to identify what you would want to be said about you during your eulogy for each core focus area of your life. This will help you gain a long-term vision of who you want to be and what you want to become in your life.

Scan To Download the Lifetime Visualizer™ Tool

THE 7 FS MATRIX™: BUILDING YOUR LIFE VISION

A well-rounded life vision requires balance. The **7 Fs,** your Faith, Fitness, Family, Focus, Finances, Friends, and Fun, represent the core areas of life that contribute to a fulfilling existence. By defining your vision in each of these areas, you create a holistic roadmap for success. The first step in developing your Lifetime Visualizer picture is to outline what you'd want to be said about you during your eulogy in each of these 7 Fs core life priority areas:

1. **Faith** – Your spiritual beliefs, values, and practices.
    - **Example**: *"He lived a life anchored in unshakable faith, guided by his values and grounded in his beliefs. His trust in God shaped every choice he made and every person he touched."*

2. **Fitness** – Your physical health and overall well-being.
    - **Example**: *"She honored the gift of her body by living with discipline, energy, and vitality. Her example reminded us that health is not just for ourselves but for the people who count on us."*

3. **Family** – Your relationships with loved ones and the legacy you want to leave.
    - **Example**: *"He was the rock and heart of his family, leading with love, laughter, and unwavering devotion. His legacy is woven into every life he helped shape and every memory he left behind."*

4. **Focus (Work)** – Your career, business, or educational goals.
    - **Example**: *"She pursued her work with passion and purpose, leaving an indelible mark on her field. Her excellence was never just for achievement's sake but to serve and create value for others."*

5. **Finances** – Your financial resources, savings, and investments.
    - **Example**: *"He was a wise steward of his resources, building security not only for himself but for generations to come. His generosity proved that true wealth is measured in impact, not just income."*

6. **Friends** – Your social connections and relationships.
    - **Example**: *"He had the rare gift of making everyone feel seen, heard, and valued. His friendships were a source of joy and strength that will be deeply missed."*

7. **Fun** – Your hobbies, interests, and passions.
    - **Example**: *"She approached life with a playful spirit and an open heart, always making time for adventure. Her laughter and love for living reminded us all that joy is worth pursuing every day."*

These are some generalized examples. As you write your eulogy statement for each of these core focus areas, you can get even more specific to your situation and your desired outcomes.

Once you've written your eulogy vision statements for each of the 7 Fs, you've painted a vivid picture of how you want to be remembered in every area of life. But vision without action is only wishful thinking. The next step is to transform these visions into **key commitments**—clear, guiding promises you make to yourself that shape your daily priorities. These commitments serve as your compass, ensuring that each decision, habit, and investment of time aligns with the legacy you want to leave.

Your eulogy vision statements define *who you want to be remembered as.* Your key commitments define *how you will live now* to make that vision a reality. They act as anchors in your life focus, keeping you steady in storms and intentional in calm waters. Over time, these commitments will influence your habits, your mindset, and even the opportunities you pursue. Below are future-focused commitments for each of the 7 Fs, written to bridge your vision into action.

Faith – Your spiritual beliefs, values, and practices.
- Example: "I will cultivate a daily meditation practice and contribute to my community through acts of service."

Fitness – Your physical health and overall well-being.
- Example: "I will maintain a healthy lifestyle, run a marathon by age forty, and practice yoga regularly."

Family – Your relationships with loved ones and the legacy you want to leave.
- Example: "I will be a devoted spouse and parent, creating a home filled with love and encouragement."

Focus (Work) – Your career, business, or educational goals.
- Example: "I will build a purpose-driven business that makes a meaningful impact in my industry."

Finances – Your financial resources, savings, and investments.
- Example: "I will achieve financial independence by fifty, allowing me to give generously and enjoy life fully."

Friends – Your social connections and relationships.
- Example: "I will cultivate deep, meaningful friendships and invest time in my community."

Fun – Your hobbies, interests, and passions.
- Example: "I will travel to thirty countries, learn a musical instrument, and regularly engage in creative pursuits."

For each of these areas, write down your **lifetime desired outcomes**. Be personal, specific, and aspirational. State each of these desired outcomes in the form of the Lifetime Visualizer. This will give you a guiding framework that helps align your daily actions with your long-term vision.

Here are some steps in crafting your vision:

1. Review your eulogy exercise using the 7 Fs Matrix™ and use it to gain a clear picture of your lifetime desired outcomes.

2. Craft a long-term vision for your life using the Vision Clarifier tool.
3. Use the Lifetime Visualizer and Vision Clarifier to articulate this vision.
4. Add these items to your Vision-Execution Snapshot, outlined later in this book.

CRAFTING YOUR LONG-TERM VISION

Once you have clarity about your purpose and values, and you have your lifetime vision, the next step is to create a vision statement for your life. Your vision statement is a vivid picture of the future you want to build. It serves as both a compass and a motivator, helping you stay focused and inspired.

VISION STATEMENTS

A vision statement is a concise declaration of your ideal life. It should reflect your purpose, values, and long-term aspirations. Here are three templates you can use as inspiration to help you draft your own personal vision statement:

Vision Statement Template 1 – "Identity → Action → Impact"

"I am becoming [your ideal self-description] by [specific actions, disciplines, or priorities]. I create a life where [describe the environment, values, or experiences you are cultivating], and I leave a legacy of [describe the difference you want to make or how you will be remembered]."

Example:

"I am becoming a wise and courageous mentor by pursuing lifelong learning, deep relationships, and unwavering integrity. I create a life where my faith anchors every decision, my family thrives, and my work makes a lasting impact. I leave a legacy of helping others see their worth and step boldly into their potential."

**Vision Statement Template 2 –
"Who I Am → How I Live → What Others Experience"**

"I choose to be [core identity or role] who [consistent action or mindset]. I live each day with [key values or guiding principles], so that [describe the positive effect on others or the world]."

Example:

"I choose to be a disciplined and joyful builder of people who listens deeply and acts with purpose. I live each day with gratitude, integrity, and resilience so that those around me feel empowered to grow, take risks, and live without fear."

**Vision Statement Template 3 –
"Purpose → Practice → Presence"**

"My purpose is to [state your deeper purpose] by [describe ongoing actions or commitments]. I create a presence that [describe the emotional, spiritual, or practical effect you have on your environment], and I am remembered for [legacy or enduring impact]."

Example:

"My purpose is to lead and love well by intentionally developing my faith, health, and relationships. I create a presence that brings peace, clarity, and encouragement wherever I go, and

I am remembered for lifting others higher than they thought they could go."

TRANSLATING VISION INTO ACTIONABLE GOALS

A vision without action is just a dream. To make your vision a reality, you need to break your Vision Blueprint™ down into actionable goals. Start by chunking your vision down into a 10-Year Vision, a 3-Year Vision, and then 1-Year Goals. Each longer-term vision will inform what your near-term vision should be. Here is how that looks from a practical basis:

- **10-Year Vision:** This is the big picture. If nothing held you back—no distractions, no delays—what would be true of your life in a decade?
- **3-Year Vision:** These are stepping stones. What needs to be true by year three to make that 10-Year Vision real? These are major milestones, not minor habits.
- **1-Year Goals:** This is where action starts. What can be built, changed, or improved in the next 12 months that directly supports the 3-Year Vision?

Example: If your 10-Year Vision for fitness is to run an ultra-marathon, your goals might look like this.

> **3-Year Vision:** Train and complete a marathon and improve endurance with structured training.
>
> **1-Year Goals:** Train and run a half-marathon and build a sustainable training routine.

By breaking down your vision into tangible goals, you create a step-by-step roadmap that ensures progress is made consistently. When you've broken down your vision into 1-Year Goals, that data will inform what quarterly objectives you'll need to create to get there.

WHY UNDERSTANDING YOUR DNA AND VISION MATTERS

Your **DNA**, which consists of your purpose, values, and natural strengths, plays a crucial role in shaping your vision. When your goals align with your core identity, you build a sustainable path to success that resonates with who you are.

Benefits of Defining Your DNA and Vision:

- **Clarity:** Knowing your purpose eliminates distractions and ensures focus on what matters.
- **Motivation:** A compelling vision fuels intrinsic motivation, making it easier to stay committed.
- **Alignment:** Your values guide your decision-making, leading to consistent, fulfilling progress.
- **Accountability:** A structured vision provides benchmarks for measuring success and maintaining accountability.

By defining your purpose, values, and vision, you create a blueprint for a fulfilling life. This clarity helps you prioritize what truly matters and align your actions with your aspirations. As you chunk your vision into actionable steps and build habits to support them, you set yourself up for long-term success.

Scan To Download the Vision Clarifier Tool™

SECTION SUMMARY: VISION

KEY INSIGHTS

Vision as a Roadmap: A clear vision guides decisions, aligns daily actions, and provides motivation, like a flight plan for a pilot.

Clarity and Specificity: Clearly defining your vision with detailed goals significantly increases your likelihood of success.

Incremental Goals: Long-term visions are best achieved by breaking them into short-term, measurable milestones.

The Power of Thinking Big: Daily disciplined execution of healthy habits and actions compound over time into results people can't imagine today. Don't let your vision be limited based on your current circumstances.

Visualization for Success: Vividly imagining success in detail enhances performance and resilience in facing challenges.

Holistic Life Balance: A well-defined vision should include all major life areas, represented by the 7 Fs: Faith, Fitness, Family, Focus (Work), Finances, Friends, and Fun.

Legacy Focused: Defining your legacy through visualization exercises helps clarify what truly matters in the long term.

Alignment with Core Identity (DNA): Goals must align with your purpose, values, and natural strengths to sustain motivation and fulfillment.

ACTIONABLE STEPS

1. **Craft Your Long-Term Vision**
   - Use tools like the Lifetime Visualizer and Vision Clarifier.
   - Write a concise Vision Statement that reflects your purpose, values, and aspirations.

2. **Define Specific Milestones**
   - Develop a 10-Year Vision outlining major life accomplishments.
   - Create a 3-Year Vision with clear, measurable milestones.
   - Set 1-Year Goals to serve as stepping stones towards your 3-year objectives.

3. **Visualize Regularly**
   - Implement consistent visualization practices to mentally rehearse achieving your goals.

4. **7 Fs Framework (Lifetime Visualizer)**
   - Clearly articulate your vision across all core life areas: Faith, Fitness, Family, Focus, Finances, Friends, and Fun.
   - Ensure balance and clarity in each domain, identifying specific, aspirational outcomes.

5. **Regular Evaluation and Adjustment**
    - Review and recalibrate your vision periodically to stay aligned and motivated.
    - Use quarterly goals, weekly objectives, and daily habits to ensure consistent progress.

By following these steps, you create a structured, actionable framework that transforms your long-term vision into an achievable reality.

After completing this section, update your Vision Execution Snapshot so it reflects what you just clarified and stays current and aligned.

PART 4

GOALS

Goals transform your vision into actionable steps. They create structure, focus, and measurable targets you can pursue with intention. Clear goals eliminate uncertainty and help you channel your energy into consistent progress, ensuring every action moves you closer to your desired outcomes.

10

GOALS: THE BRIDGE BETWEEN VISION AND REALITY

Excuses are comfortable—until the bill arrives. Get JACKED, pay the price in discipline, and cash out in freedom.

In the Personal Success System, goals are where clarity becomes movement. This is the stage where the lofty, energizing ideas of your Vision and the core convictions of your DNA get translated into tangible, measurable outcomes. In other words, goals are the bridge between who you are (DNA), where you're going (Vision), and what you're doing now (Goals)—they aren't arbitrary checkpoints but intentionally engineered mile markers guiding the journey.

WHY GOALS MATTER

Without goals, your Vision remains a dream. Misaligned or vague goals can become distractions—productive, perhaps, but not purposeful. Clear, compelling, and purpose-driven goals offer:

- **Direction** – guiding where to focus effort
- **Focus** – enabling a meaningful "yes" to what matters and a "no" to distractions
- **Motivation** – providing reasons to persist when the going gets tough
- **Feedback** – acting as a scoreboard to track progress and recalibrate

Put simply: if Vision is the compass, Goals are the map.

GOAL-SETTING EFFECTIVENESS

Research consistently shows that setting *specific, challenging* goals yields better performance than vague or easy goals.[80] Hard goals outperform easy ones—but only when they remain believable and achievable.[81] Written business plans, which reflect specificity and alignment, are linked with notably faster company growth.[82] Yet setting overly high goals has pitfalls: since high-goal standards often mean only about 10 percent can reach them, 90 percent face failure—potentially decreasing motivation and self-esteem.[83]

NEUROSCIENCE OF GOAL PURSUIT

Neurological research highlights that both motivational ("will") and cognitive ("way") aspects are integral to goal pursuit, with executive functions (like attention and working memory) playing critical roles; and with time, goal behaviors become more automatized and habitual.

STRATEGY EXECUTION CHALLENGES

Strategy implementation often falters due to poor execution: unclear roles, vague priorities, and ineffective communication are common issues.

ENHANCING GOAL EXECUTION

Effective execution strategies include deploying frameworks like a PSS for consistent goal clarity and progress measurement, as well as incorporating reinforcement learning models that account for goal-dependent (intrinsic) rewards.

Goals are essential in the Quit Jacking Around Personal Success System, functioning as the bridge from Vision to Action. Through direction, focus, motivation, and feedback, goals transform purpose into progress.

Research confirms that specific, challenging—but achievable—goals drive superior performance, while overly lofty goals risk demotivation or failure.

Neuroscience underlines that successful goal pursuit blends motivation ("will") and cognitive planning ("way"), and over time, these behaviors can become automated.

Strategic pitfalls arise mostly from poor execution—unclear responsibilities, misaligned priorities, and ineffective communication.

Effective frameworks like your Personal Success System and models emphasizing intrinsic rewards improve execution quality.

Technological tools enhance this further—AI wizards, monitoring platforms, and collaboration software streamline goal setting, tracking, and alignment in real time.

STATING GOALS IN A POSITIVE TENSE

The way we articulate our goals—especially in the present and positive tense—can make the difference between wishful thinking and measurable achievement. This is not just motivational fluff; it's grounded in decades of research across neuroscience, cognitive psychology, and behavioral science. The words you use to speak to yourself literally change the way your brain processes information, stores memory, and makes decisions.[84]

When you consistently phrase goals as if they are already happening—"I am a disciplined leader" instead of "I will be a disciplined leader"—you train your brain to operate as though the outcome is part of your current identity. This mental shift moves your goal from something distant to something you already embody, creating an internal pressure to act in alignment with that identity.

Neuroscientific Basis:

Brain Activation and Neuroplasticity

When you state your goals in a positive tense, you activate specific brain systems associated with self-processing, motivation, and reward, particularly the ventral striatum (VS) and the ventral medial prefrontal cortex (VMPFC).[85] These areas are crucial for assigning value to your own actions and reinforcing behaviors that move you toward your objectives.

This process is reinforced by neuroplasticity, the brain's ability to form and strengthen neural pathways over time. Repeated affirmations act like mental "reps" in a gym—each repetition strengthens the neural circuits related to confidence, resilience, and goal-oriented thinking.[86] Over time, your default thought patterns shift toward possibility and persistence rather than self-doubt and hesitation.

Interestingly, neuroscience has also shown that the brain responds to vividly imagined scenarios much like it does to actual experiences. That means pairing affirmations with visualization can cause your brain to "pre-experience" success, reducing performance anxiety and increasing the likelihood of follow-through.[87]

Emotional Regulation and Stress Reduction

Affirmations can downregulate brain activity in the amygdala, the region associated with fear, stress, and threat detection.[88] By decreasing the intensity of your body's stress response, positive self-statements make it easier to stay calm and focused, especially in high-pressure situations. This matters because stress is not only a distraction—it can impair the prefrontal cortex, the brain's decision-making hub.

This is why top athletes, elite military units, and high-stakes leaders train themselves to control inner dialogue: keeping the brain in a calm, resourceful state allows for better strategy and execution under pressure

Psychological Impact:

Self-Perception and Confidence

Self-affirmation theory suggests that humans are motivated to preserve a positive self-image.[89] When you repeatedly tell yourself, "I am resourceful and capable," your mind begins to interpret incoming information through that lens. This has a compounding effect—confidence leads to more action, action leads to results, and results reinforce confidence.

This isn't about ignoring flaws or pretending to be perfect. It's about intentionally amplifying constructive beliefs so that they outweigh destructive ones. As PositivePsychology.com notes, affirmations can serve as a psychological "reset button," helping you shift perspective after setbacks.[90]

Cognitive Restructuring

From a cognitive-behavioral standpoint, affirmations help with **cognitive restructuring**—the process of identifying, challenging, and replacing harmful thought patterns. By inserting a deliberate, positive statement, you interrupt the automatic loop of negative self-talk and redirect it toward something more constructive.[91]

Over time, this reduces the mental energy wasted on doubt, shame, and second-guessing, freeing up focus for problem-solving and creative thinking.

Keys to Goal Achievement and Performance

Focus and Motivation

Affirmations work like mental "goal posts," constantly reorienting your attention toward what matters most. The more you repeat and internalize them, the more your brain filters distractions and highlights opportunities aligned with your objective.[92]

This is supported by the **Reticular Activating System (RAS)**—a network in your brainstem that acts like a filter for sensory information. If your affirmation is, "I see opportunities for growth in every challenge," your RAS begins to spot and flag those opportunities in real life, making your environment feel more possibility-rich.

Athletic Performance

In sports psychology, positive self-talk has been linked to increased endurance, better technical execution, and faster skill acquisition.[93] This principle applies far beyond athletics. Whether you're closing a business deal, giving a presentation, or running a marathon, your self-talk influences your performance under pressure.

Practical Implementation

To maximize the effectiveness of affirmations and goal statements:

1. **Frame in the present tense** – Speak as though the goal is already achieved ("I am financially disciplined" vs. "I will save money").[94]

2. **Be specific and emotionally resonant** – Vague affirmations have little impact; specificity makes them believable and actionable.[95]
3. **Repeat consistently** – Especially in moments of doubt, repetition reinforces the neural pathways you want to strengthen.[96]
4. **Pair with visualization** – Picture the goal vividly to engage more of your brain's sensory and emotional systems.[97]
5. **Anchor to daily triggers** – Tie affirmations to existing habits (e.g., say them during your morning coffee or while brushing your teeth) to make them automatic.

By harnessing the neuroscience of affirmation, the psychology of self-perception, and the behavioral science of habit formation, you can rewire your mental operating system for success. Positive, present-tense goal statements are more than optimistic words—they are cognitive tools for building the identity, confidence, and focus required to achieve meaningful results.

THE JACKED FRAMEWORK™: QUIT JACKING AROUND AND ACHIEVE YOUR GOALS

SETTING BETTER GOALS WITH THE PERSONAL SUCCESS SYSTEM

When you're ready to quit jacking around and finally make real progress, you need a goal-setting system that's smart, practical, and a little irreverent. Enter The JACKED Framework—a no-nonsense, memorable acronym to Justify, Assess, Create, Knock Out, Execute, and Drive your way to success.

This framework is rooted in proven goal-setting principles (you'll notice echoes of classic models like GROW and SMART, with our own twist) but delivers them with the punchy tone of *Quit Jacking Around*. Use this as your personal roadmap to set powerful goals, plan effectively, and stay motivated. Let's get JACKED!

OVERVIEW OF JACKED COMPONENTS

- **J – Justify Your Goal:** Define exactly what you want to achieve and why it truly matters. This is your compelling purpose behind the goal, the fuel that will keep you going when things get tough. Be specific. What does a successful outcome look like, and when do you plan to achieve it? Ensure it aligns with your values and long-term vision. *If you can't clearly justify the goal to yourself, it's easy to lose focus.* Include the positive payoff of hitting this goal and even the cost of not taking action (so you know what's at stake).

- **A – Assess Your Reality:** Take an honest look at where you're starting. Where are you right now in relation to your goal? What strengths, resources, and skills can you leverage? What challenges or gaps do you face? This reality check sets the baseline. A smart planner identifies current obstacles and limitations early, without judgment, so you know what you're working with. A clear assessment prevents wishful thinking and grounds your plan in reality, helping you be practical and prepared.

- **C – Create Your Winning Plan:** Now, brainstorm and outline how you'll get from where you are to where you want to be. Consider options and strategies. What are all the possible ways to reach your goal? Get creative and list multiple approaches. Also, think about *who* or *what* can help: mentors, partners, tools, or systems you can enlist. What new habits could you establish to support your progress? At this stage, generate ideas freely (at least 3–5 strategies or action ideas), then choose the most promising path or combination of actions. In short, chart a course toward your goal by selecting a strategy that plays to your strengths and resources. Remember, there's often more than one way to the finish line; your job is to create a roadmap that excites you and feels achievable.

- **K – Knock Out Obstacles:** Don't wait for challenges to ambush you; anticipate them *in advance*. Identify the potential obstacles, roadblocks, and even internal opposition (like fear or limiting beliefs) that could hinder your plan. Maybe it's a lack of time, financial constraints, self-doubt, procrastination, or unsupportive environments; get it all on the table. For each obstacle, plot out a counter-attack. How will you overcome it or prevent it from derailing you? For example, if you tend to lose motivation, you might schedule weekly check-ins with an accountability partner. If you foresee budget issues, maybe one of your "Create" strategies is finding low-cost alternatives. By knocking out obstacles before they knock you out, you transform excuses into action items. This step is about building resilience into your plan, so when life throws a punch, you're ready to punch back. *(Tip: Also address any nagging negative self-talk. Identify those limiting beliefs and flip them into empowering truths that keep you moving forward.)*

- **E – Execute with Excellence:** A goal without action is just a daydream. It's time to convert your plan into concrete action steps and commit to executing them. Take your chosen strategy and break it down into specific tasks and milestones. Assign deadlines to each milestone;

dates keep you accountable and prevent procrastination. Ensure each action step is crystal clear and measurable so you can track progress.

In the JACKED Framework, we adapt SMART goals to include an extra criterion, favoring action plans that are SMAART (Specific, Measurable, Achievable, Aspirational, Relevant, Time-bound) without bogging you down in jargon. In plain terms: Know exactly what you need to do, know how you'll measure success, and double-check that your plan is realistic and aligned with your larger purpose. Set time frames for each step.

For example, instead of saying, "I'll get in shape soon," your execution plan might state, "I will jog for thirty minutes, three times a week, and prepare home-cooked meals five days a week, starting tomorrow." Organize your steps in a simple action plan, table, or list. (See the Tool section for a template.) Make sure to include resources or support you'll use for each step, whether it's a workout app, a class, or a friend who agreed to help.

The Execute stage is all about translating your dream into doable chunks and then taking the first step immediately. Once your plan is laid out, *take action!* Don't wait for perfect conditions; start executing the first task on your list. Momentum builds motivation.

- **D – Drive It Home (Dedicate and Deliver):** This final step is about maintaining your determination and following through until you hit that goal. It's not a one-time action; it's a mindset of commitment. First, double down on your *why*. Take a moment to vividly picture the success payoff of achieving your goal. How will life be better? How will you feel? Who else will benefit? Remind yourself of the risk of inaction. What do you lose by giving up or delaying? This boosts your resolve on hard days.

Next, set up a system to track your progress and keep yourself accountable over time. You might use a habit tracker, journal, or have weekly progress meetings with yourself.

Regularly review what's working and what isn't. Did you hit this week's milestone? If yes, celebrate it. Give yourself credit for every bit of progress; motivation thrives on recognition. If not, analyze why. Maybe your approach needs tweaking. That's okay; adjust the plan rather than abandoning it.

Stay adaptable, and be willing to implement your Plan B from those other options you brainstormed if needed. The Drive stage is essentially *rinse-and-repeat:* keep executing your action steps, monitor results, and make corrections until you cross the finish line. Through consistent dedication, you'll turn your plan into a reality.

Remember, the only time you truly fail is when you quit, so keep driving forward, and don't let up until you've delivered on your goal.

EXAMPLE: APPLYING JACKED TO A PERSONAL GOAL

To see how the JACKED Framework works in real life, let's apply it to an example goal—say, losing 20 pounds by December 31.

- **Justify (J):** Lose 20 pounds by the end of the year.

   Why: to improve my health and energy, and to feel confident in my body. It aligns with my value of living a long, active life for my family. If I don't do this, I risk further weight gain, potential health issues, and lower self-esteem. Clearly, the stakes are high enough to keep me motivated!

- **Assess (A):** Current weight is 200 pounds, with a busy desk job and no regular exercise. I have knowledge of nutrition from past dieting, and I'm injury-free (that's a strength!). Challenges: I'm often drained after work, and I tend to snack on junk food when stressed. My reality check: I need to build more activity into my week and plan my meals to overcome these habits.

- **Create (C):** Possible strategies to achieve this goal:
    1. Join a gym and follow a structured three-day-a-week workout program.
    2. Meal plan every Sunday to prepare healthy lunches and dinners.
    3. Wake up 30 minutes earlier for a morning walk or jog.
    4. Ask a friend to be an accountability buddy and exercise with me.

   I decide my winning plan will combine a few of these. I'll do strength training at the gym on Monday, Wednesday, and Friday, walk on other days, stick to a meal plan, and check in with my friend weekly. I'll also use a calorie-tracking app for accountability.

- **Knock Out (K):** Obstacles I anticipate.

  Time—Sometimes work or family duties cut into exercise time. (Solution: Schedule workouts like appointments on my calendar, and have a 20-minute backup workout for busy days).

  Motivation dips—I know there will be days I won't *feel* like exercising, or I'll crave junk food. (Solution: Keep a visible reminder of my *why*, like a photo that represents a healthy future. Allow myself one planned treat meal a week so I don't feel deprived.)

  Holiday season temptations—Big obstacles! (Solution: Plan smaller portions and healthy dishes for family gatherings. Focus on socializing more than eating.)

  By thinking these through, I'm not caught off guard later. I've also identified a limiting belief, "I've never succeeded long-term before, so maybe I just can't." I'll knock that out by replacing it with, "Past attempts taught me what *not* to do. This time I'm equipped, and I deserve to succeed." My new mantra: *I am capable of change, one day at a time.*

- **Execute (E):** I break the big goal into milestones: for example, lose about two pounds a month.

  Specific action steps:

  Daily: follow my meal plan (around 1,800 calories per day) and do at least thirty minutes of activity.

Weekly: three gym sessions (Monday, Wednesday, and Friday at 6 p.m.), two runs (Tuesday and Thursday mornings), weigh in every Sunday to track progress.

By month three: lose about 10 pounds (halfway mark). Reward myself with new running shoes.

By month six: hit 20 pounds down. Celebrate with a weekend hiking trip!

I mark the calendar with these targets and share them with my friend, so I can't easily back out. I've ensured the plan is achievable (two pounds a month is reasonable) and aligned with my life. I've chosen activities I enjoy, slotted them into my schedule, time-bound, with clear deadlines.

Resources in play: my food-tracking app, a gym membership, and support from my friends and family. Now, it's go time. I start today by doing my first workout and grocery shopping for healthy meals.

- **Drive (D):** To keep myself accountable, I set up a progress journal. Every Sunday, I record my weight and reflect. Did I stick to the plan this week? I'll answer questions. "What went well? What challenges came up? What will I do next week to improve?"

  If I lost weight, fantastic—that fuels my fire. If not, I'll troubleshoot. Maybe I need to adjust my calorie intake or try a new workout class if boredom is an issue. I also revisit my "why" often. I imagine playing soccer with my kids, with new energy and no back pain. This is *hugely* motivating.

When fatigue tempts me to skip a workout, I remind myself, "Skipping isn't worth the setback. I'd rather feel proud tomorrow." I've even put a sticky note on my mirror, *"No excuses. No quitting. You've got this!"*

Each small win, like resisting cake at the office or dropping another pound, gets a mini celebration. I'll blast my favorite song or tell my friend about it. These practices keep my determination high. By the end of the year, as I step on the scale and see 180 pounds, I'll know that staying driven made the difference. You can bet I'll be celebrating that victory!

The example above shows how JACKED comes to life for a fitness goal, but this framework works for any goal: career, personal projects, financial, you name it. The key is to honestly engage with each step. Now it's your turn to get JACKED about your goals!

Scan To Download the JACKED Framework™ Tool

THE POWER OF QUARTERLY GOALS

One of the biggest problems people face with goal setting is biting off more than they can chew. That's why Quarterly Goals are a game-changer. They allow you to move quickly without being overwhelmed.

Each quarter becomes a focused sprint where you take intentional action toward your 1-Year Goals. At the end of each quarter, you assess.

- What progress did I make?
- What did I learn?
- What needs to change for the next quarter?

This rhythm builds consistency, agility, and confidence. You're not here to drift through life, hoping things work out. You're here to make an impact. That means you must move with intention.

Goals are your declaration that you're done jacking around. Your time, energy, and focus are too valuable to waste. You're building a life that matters, one goal, one quarter, one day at a time.

So don't just dream, and don't just plan. Set the goal. Start the work. See it through.

CLARIFYING YOUR QUARTERLY GOALS WITH THE JACKED FRAMEWORK

Having established your purpose, values, and vision, you now hold the blueprint for the life you want to build. However, vision without execution is still just a daydream. The **JACKED Framework** turns that dream into decisive action and clear quarterly wins.

Why Quarterly?

A twelve-week horizon is long enough to achieve meaningful progress yet short enough to maintain urgency and focus. Each quarter becomes a sprint toward your bigger annual objectives, an ideal cadence for reflection, celebration, and course-correction.

JACKED GOAL-SETTING ACTION STEPS

- → **Break** your 1-year goals into quarterly objectives and bite-sized daily and weekly actions.
- → **Apply JACKED** to create clarity, context, and commitment for every quarterly goal.
- → **Translate** the framework into concrete, trackable commitments (see the Tool for tables and templates).

Establish Key Performance Indicators (KPIs) that let you measure progress at a glance.

TRANSLATING ANNUAL GOALS INTO QUARTERLY OBJECTIVES

Your annual goals serve as the roadmap; quarterly goals are the mile-markers. Systematic, 90-day planning lets you focus on what matters now while keeping you aligned with the longer journey.

Example – Annual Savings Goal

Annual Target:
Save $20,000 this year.

Quarter	Focus	Target Amount	Key Actions
Q1	Lay the Foundation	$5,000	Audit spending, cut discretionary expenses, launch a side hustle
Q2	Accelerate	$5,000	Automate transfers, raise income (rate increase, new client, overtime)
Q3	Optimize and Adjust	$5,000	Review budget, refine side hustle pricing, address obstacles
Q4	Finish Strong	$5,000	Maintain momentum, celebrate milestones, complete year-end audit

Total Saved = **$20,000**

The JACKED Framework (Quarterly Focus Edition)

Step	Core Questions	Quarterly Application
J – Justify	*What exactly do I want, and why must I achieve it this quarter?*	Craft a vivid goal statement for the next ninety days and record the positive payoff (and cost of inaction).
A – Assess	*Where am I starting? What resources, strengths, and gaps define my current reality?*	Review last quarter's metrics; list assets you can leverage and obstacles already on the radar.

C – Create	*What strategies and support systems can get me to the finish line?*	Brainstorm at least three approaches, select the winning plan, map milestones inside the quarter.
K – Knock Out	*What could derail me, and how will I neutralize it in advance?*	Identify external barriers (time, money) and internal barriers (beliefs, habits). Pair each with a counter-measure.
E – Execute	*What specific, measurable actions happen this week and next?*	Convert strategy into weekly sprints with deadlines, KPIs, and accountability touchpoints.
D – Drive	*How will I track, review, and adapt until the goal is won?*	Schedule weekly reviews, celebrate wins, adjust tactics, and recommit to "the why."

Justify • Assess • Create • Knock Out • Execute • Drive

EXAMPLE – APPLYING JACKED TO Q1 SAVINGS ($5,000)

Justify – *Goal:* Save $5,000 by March 31. *Why:* Build an emergency fund and reduce stress. *Payoff:* Peace of mind; option to seize investment opportunities. *Risk of inaction:* Continued financial anxiety.

Assess – Current savings is $0; disposable income is $300 per month; unused subscriptions total $120 per month; overtime opportunity is available.

Create – Strategies: (a) cancel subscriptions, (b) trim dining-out to once per week, (c) pick up two freelance projects. Implement all three strategies.

Knock Out – Obstacles: impulse buys

- ➢ → install a spending-freeze app
- ➢ → fatigue after work
- ➢ → block Sunday morning for freelancing

Limiting belief: "I never stick to budgets." Replacement truth: "Every dollar has a job, and I'm the boss."

Execute – Action Plan:

- Cancel subscriptions by January 10 (saves $120 per month).
- Meal prep Sundays (cuts grocery bill by $60 per week).
- Book first freelance gig by January 20 (aim for $1,000 net per month).
- KPI: Track weekly net savings in a spreadsheet.

Drive – Weekly

Friday money check-in: reward every $1,000 saved with a small, planned treat (under $50).

- Adjust tactics mid-quarter if KPIs slip.

FROM CLARITY TO SPECIFICITY

The JACKED Framework naturally embeds the attributes of a *Specific, Measurable, Achievable, Aligned, Relevant, and Time-bound* commitment during **Execute**.

Think of JACKED as the engine and these attributes as the spark plugs. Together, they convert raw intention into disciplined action.

Pro-Tip: When you write your Justify statement, *start with the deadline*. Then work backward through Assess, Create, Knock-out, and Execute. Finish by Driving momentum with weekly reviews. This reverse-engineering keeps the end in sight and the path unmistakably clear.

READY TO GET JACKED?

1. Print the accompanying **JACKED Tool.**
2. Fill it out for each quarterly goal.
3. Keep the Tool visible. Review it at least once a week.
4. Momentum is built on small, consistent wins.
5. Stack them, and the big prize takes care of itself.
6. Quit jacking around. Get JACKED!
7. Drive your goals home, one focused quarter at a time.

11

ESTABLISHING HABITS AND ACTIONS: TURNING VISION INTO REALITY ONE DAY AT A TIME

FROM VISION TO ACTION: THE FLOW OF EXECUTION

You've done the hard work of thinking big. You've wrestled with purpose, clarified your values, envisioned your future, and translated that into tangible goals. You've zoomed in from your 10-Year Vision to your 3-Year Vision, down to your 1-Year Goals, and then your Quarterly Goals. By now, you can see the road ahead more clearly than ever before.

But here's the truth that trips up more people than anything else: **clarity without consistent action is just a dream with a nice map.**

I've coached countless people who had no shortage of vision or strategy, but their execution fell apart because they never built the daily rhythms to bring it to life. They didn't fail because they lacked the ability. They failed because they treated their vision like a destination they could teleport to instead of a mountain they had to climb—step by step, day by day.

The Personal Success System is not about one-time sprints or sporadic bursts of effort. It's about building a way of living where your daily and weekly actions naturally stack toward your long-term vision. Every component of the system flows downward into the next until it finally lands in the smallest, most powerful unit of change: your habits.

Think of it like a cascading waterfall:

1. **Purpose and Values** shape the way you make every decision.
2. **A 10-Year Vision** gives you a clear destination.
3. **A 3-Year Vision** outlines your map.
4. **1-Year Goals** mark your major milestones.
5. **Quarterly Goals** define your next 90-day outcomes.
6. **Weekly Focuses** align your attention with intention.
7. **Daily Actions and Habits** are where the rubber meets the road.

When someone misses a quarterly goal, it almost always traces back to inconsistency in the daily actions. And when someone hits a long-term goal, it's never magic; it's the reward of small, intentional choices made repeatedly, often long before the results show up.

That's why in this chapter we're going to move from **vision to action**—and not just any action, but disciplined, consistent, identity-driven habits that make success inevitable. You'll see why small daily habits matter far more than random bursts of motivation, how to design habits that actually stick, and how to track your progress so you can build momentum instead of losing it.

By the time you finish this chapter, you won't just have a plan for your habits; you'll have a system for making sure they happen, no matter what life throws at you. Because if your vision is the *why* and your goals are the *what*, your habits are the *how*. And it's the *how* that turns good intentions into a life you're proud of.

GOALS: MILESTONES, NOT DESTINATIONS

In *Quit Jacking Around*, we make a critical distinction. Goals are not finish lines painted on a wall. They're signposts along the road of perpetual growth.

When I set a goal, I'm not proclaiming, "Once I reach this, I'll rest." Instead, I'm declaring, "This is the next waypoint on my journey." Whether it's hitting a revenue target for my company, writing a book, or building stronger rhythms in my family life, each goal simply marks a moment where I pause, assess, and chart the next course forward.

Your daily and weekly habits are your steps in the journey, and your goals are the milestones on the path toward your long-term vision.

THE POWER OF HABITS AS YOUR DAILY COMPASS

If goals are the milestones, then habits are the footfalls that get you there. You don't wake up one morning and suddenly find yourself at the summit of personal or professional success. Growth happens one decision at a time.

That daily five-minute journal, that weekly review of your KPI dashboard, that consistent date night on your calendar, these small actions build momentum and keep you pointed toward your next milestone.

Habits are the compound interest of progress, imperceptibly small day to day, but overwhelmingly powerful over months and years.

- **Daily Habits:** Your non-negotiables: exercise, prayer or meditation, learning, and a quick review of your top three priorities.
- **Weekly Habits:** The checkpoint routines: team huddle on Monday, financial review on Wednesday, and family dinner reflection on Friday.

By weaving these habits into the fabric of your life, you create a scaffold that not only supports you in hitting each milestone but also readies you to redefine and elevate your next goal.

RECALIBRATE AND RESET

When you reach a milestone, celebrate, give thanks, reflect on what worked, and glean lessons from what didn't. Don't park there. Continuous growth demands that the moment you cross one milestone, you set your sights on the next.

Your habits don't change; the destination does. Over time, this cycle of goal setting, habit tracking, milestone celebration, and course correction becomes second nature. You'll realize that the true reward isn't the trophy at the end but the person you become on the way.

- In this system, goals fuel your forward motion, habits are the engine, and accountability ensures you keep moving. Embrace each milestone as proof of progress; then press on, with the proper habits in place, there's no limit to how far you can go.

HOW SMALL DAILY HABITS CREATE MASSIVE PERSONAL SUCCESS

You've done the foundational work, clarified your DNA (Purpose + Values), crafted a compelling 10-Year Vision, refined your 3-Year Vision, and identified the 1-Year and Quarterly Goals that align with who you are and where you're going. These elements form a powerful framework for direction and clarity, but none of them matter if you do not take consistent daily action.

Success is not the product of chance, nor is it the reward for sporadic moments of hard work. It is the compound result of what you do daily.

Transformation is not a one-time event; it is the fruit of persistent effort in the same direction guided by small, strategic behaviors repeated consistently over time.

The Quit Jacking Around Personal Success System is designed not only to clarify your long-term aspirations but to help you build the kind of life that realizes those aspirations through disciplined daily living, and that begins with habits.

WHY SMALL DAILY HABITS MATTER MORE THAN MOTIVATION

Motivation is unreliable. It is fleeting, emotional, and circumstantial. Some days you'll feel driven and energized; other days you won't.

Waiting for motivation to act is a losing strategy.

The most successful people are not the ones who are always motivated. They are the ones who have built structures into their daily lives that guide their behavior, especially on the hard days. That structure is built on habits.

A habit is a behavior you perform automatically or with minimal resistance because it has been repeated often enough to become a part of your subconscious rhythm. It reduces cognitive load, minimizes decision fatigue, and allows you to focus your energy on meaningful progress.

This is why small habits matter. They are manageable, sustainable, and repeatable. They remove friction. They reduce resistance, and over time, they generate results that far exceed their initial effort.

THE LAW OF COMPOUNDING BEHAVIOR

Often, people underestimate the power of consistent effort over time. They want instant success. They want overnight results, but life doesn't work that way.

One small action performed daily may seem insignificant, but over a year or a decade, its effect compounds. For example:

> Flossing one tooth takes less than thirty seconds. Doing it every day builds a dental hygiene habit that prevents painful and costly health issues.
> Writing just fifty words per day leads to an 18,000-word manuscript over a year, enough for a short book.
> Saving five dollars per day leads to a $1,825-reserve in a year. With interest and investment, this builds lifelong financial discipline.

The principle is simple: small, consistent actions deliver exponential returns. They may seem invisible at first, but their results become undeniable over time.

BUILDING IDENTITY-ALIGNED HABITS

THE PATH TO REAL SUCCESS IS DAILY ACTION, REPEATED WITH DISCIPLINE, ALIGNED WITH PURPOSE.

Your habits must reflect your identity. When your actions are aligned with who you believe yourself to be, they become easier to maintain.

If your identity is vague or disconnected from your purpose, habits become harder to sustain. When you internalize the belief "This is who I am," your actions become an extension of your character.

Instead of setting a habit to work out every day, define yourself as the kind of person who honors your body. Instead of simply saying you want to save money, believe that you are a wise and intentional steward of your resources.

Every time you follow through on a habit, you cast a vote for your future self. You reinforce your identity. You build confidence, and you increase the likelihood that the behavior will continue.

This is why the Personal Success System is not just a productivity framework. It's a personal formation system. It helps you become who you were created to be, not just do more things.

THE STRUCTURE OF A HABIT

> Change might not be fast and it isn't always easy.
> But with time and effort, almost any habit can be reshaped.
> —*Charles Duhigg*

In his book, *The Power of Habit*, Charles Duhigg focuses on the structure of habits and how to change them.[98]

He asserts that every habit is built around a neurological loop consisting of three components:

> Cue: The trigger that signals the start of the habit
> Routine: The behavior or action itself
> Reward: The benefit that reinforces the behavior and makes you want to repeat it

To build new habits, you must consciously design each part of this loop.

> Cue: Anchor the habit to an existing routine or environmental trigger.

Routine: Make the behavior as easy and frictionless as possible to begin.

Reward: Reinforce the behavior immediately with something positive or meaningful.

Example:

Cue: Pouring your morning coffee

Routine: Open your planner and review your top three priorities for the day

Reward: A sense of clarity and purpose before the workday begins

When this loop is repeated daily, it becomes automatic. You no longer have to think about it. You simply do it. Use this information to understand how to build habits that work in the daily and weekly steps you execute to accomplish your goal.

DESIGNING YOUR HABIT SYSTEM WITH THE PSS HABIT FRAMEWORK

The Quit Jacking Around Habit Framework™ includes five critical design principles to ensure your habits stick and serve your greater goals.

1. **Anchor the Habit**

    Attach it to an existing routine or environment so it becomes part of your natural rhythm.

2. **Make It Tiny**

    Start with a version of the habit that is so small, it's impossible to fail. Progress begins with completion, not perfection.

3. **Reinforce Identity**

    Link the habit to the kind of person you are becoming, not just the outcome you desire.

4. **Track and Measure**

    What gets measured gets managed. Tracking builds self-awareness and accountability.

5. **Adjust Weekly**

    Use your Weekly Review to reflect on habit execution and make minor adjustments to increase effectiveness.

You don't need ten new habits. You need one keystone habit that creates momentum. Then build from there.

Duhigg also introduced the concept of **Keystone Habits**, habits that create a ripple effect across your life. For example, regular exercise improves mood, sleep, discipline, and focus.[99]

KEYSTONE HABITS: HIGH-LEVERAGE BEHAVIORS

A keystone habit is a behavior that creates positive ripple effects in multiple areas of life. It's a foundational discipline that strengthens your overall system of living.

Examples of keystone habits include:

- Daily exercise: improves energy, sleep, confidence, and stress management.
- Morning journaling: builds clarity, emotional regulation, and vision alignment.
- Budget tracking: fosters stewardship, awareness, and peace of mind.
- Prayer, meditation, or devotion: increases focus, spiritual strength, and centeredness.
- Evening review and planning: sets you up for a proactive, productive next day.

Start by identifying one keystone habit that aligns with your current goals, and build it into your morning or evening routine. Protect it like it matters, because it does.

Once you have determined your keystone habit, you can group additional habits that will systematically follow it. This combination of habits is referred to as a habit stack. Combine these habits into natural rhythms of your day to create a habit stack that will lead to accomplishing your habits together.

SAMPLE DAILY HABIT STACK

Morning Stack:

1. Keystone Habit: Drink a glass of water upon waking
2. Read a single paragraph from your Purpose or Vision Statement
3. Write one sentence expressing gratitude or reflection
4. Identify your top three priorities for the day

5. Begin the most important task of the day before checking email or messages

Evening Stack:

1. Keystone Habit: Conduct a brief review of the day's wins and lessons
2. Track progress on key habits and goals
3. Update budget or spending log
4. Write down the top task for tomorrow
5. End the day with a reflection, prayer, or moment of quiet

This entire routine can be executed in less than thirty minutes per day and will radically improve your clarity, consistency, and confidence over time. But there are always challenges to our consistency, so it is best to try to anticipate as many obstacles to our consistent and disciplined execution as possible before they happen.

ELIMINATE BARRIERS BEFORE THEY SHOW UP

One of the most underrated strategies in successful execution is removing friction before it shows up. The easier it is to take action, the more likely you are to follow through, especially when energy or motivation is low. That's why part of mastering execution is learning to *pre-decide* your success.

A simple but powerful practice is setting up your next day the night before. Before going to bed, take five minutes to write down your top three priorities for tomorrow. This single step eliminates the morning decision fog and replaces it with clarity and intention. When you wake up, you're not asking, *"What should I do today?"* You're stepping into the day already knowing what matters most.

Another powerful way to eliminate barriers is by preparing your environment for your habits. For example, when I plan to work out, I set my intention the night before by laying out my workout gear: shoes, clothes, a towel, and my pre-workout drink mix. I also decide exactly what workout I'm doing. That small act of preparation makes it easier to start because all the friction points, the decisions, the logistics, and the excuses have already been handled in advance.

ANTICIPATE ISSUES THAT MIGHT DERAIL YOUR PROGRESS

Travel, vacations, and holidays are three common areas that prevent people from achieving their goals. To avoid derailing your progress, be sure to have a plan that keeps you on course. If I'm going on vacation, I plan in advance when and how I'll work out during the trip. Just as important, I also set a clear plan for when I'll resume my regular routine after I return. Execution doesn't have to stop when life changes; it just needs to be re-planned with intention.

Whether it's a workout, a writing session, a sales call block, or your morning quiet time, success favors the prepped. When you eliminate decision points and logistical hurdles in advance, you reduce the resistance that often sabotages momentum. The path of least resistance is no longer the couch or the phone; it's the routine you've already prepared.

So don't wait until the moment to decide; *decide now*. Remove the obstacles, set the table, clear the runway. Your future self will thank you for making execution simple, inevitable, and automatic.

THE ROLE OF TRACKING

Tracking creates clarity. It allows you to see patterns and progress. Whether you use a digital habit tracker, a printed worksheet, or a calendar-based system, it creates fact-driven feedback that is critical to success. Otherwise, we evaluate progress on emotions, biased interpretations, or not at all. Visual progress increases follow-through.

When you track habits:

- You are more honest about your consistency.
- You feel motivated by visible streaks and patterns.
- You develop a feedback loop that encourages improvement.

Include a daily habit tracker in your planner or digital system. Record whether or not you executed your habits. At the end of each week, use your weekly review to assess trends, celebrate wins, and make minor adjustments. We will discuss more about tracking later in the book.

HABIT TRACKING: SO EASY A CHILD COULD DO IT

Every morning, I wake up before the sun, and I get through my workout and my morning routine. Then I head into the kitchen with a cup of coffee or tea in hand. Before I sip that first warm gulp, I take a moment to peek in on my ten-year-old son, Eli. Eli is a bright blessing in our lives, and he happens to have Down syndrome.

Once he wakes up, he greets the day with a yawn and a stretch. We get him changed, and then, without prompting, he walks over to his very own planner, his picture board. It's a simple wooden frame holding laminated cards with images of his tasks: getting the newspaper, eating breakfast, helping to unload the dishwasher, and additional morning chores. At the end of the list, his goal is clear. He sees the bright picture of himself playing his favorite video game. Each card lines up like stepping stones toward his true goal, playtime.

Eli touches the first card, "Get the newspaper." He goes with me to get it, and then moves it to the "Done" pile. His small face lights up with pride as he sees that one step behind him. The board isn't magic; it's the power of a clear plan made visible. Every time he completes a task, he gets one card closer to the play icon. More importantly, one step closer to mastering the discipline of daily habits. As a coach, a leader, and a father, I see in Eli's routine a perfect blueprint for execution: define the milestones, visualize them, and check them off one by one.

Throughout the day, Eli returns to that board each time he finishes a task. When he finishes emptying the dishwasher, he glances back at the board. When he finishes book reading time, he does the same. It's become instinctive, like a rhythm he follows without needing me to remind him. Every time he places a card into "Done," he experiences a small victory that fuels the next one. By the time he reaches the final card, the picture of him at the controller, he knows he's earned that moment of joy. He's learned that consistency and focus turn intention into action and action into progress.

Watching him, I'm reminded that execution isn't about willpower alone. It's about giving ourselves a roadmap and creating visible checkpoints along the way. Eli's picture board is simple, but its impact is profound. It turns abstract goals into tangible tasks, fuels daily momentum, and builds confidence every step of the way. If my ten-year-old son can harness this tool, so can we. Execution starts small: one task, one card, one deliberate action at a time. Before you know it, you've built a habit that carries you all the way to your vision.

WHAT TO DO WHEN YOU MISS

No one is perfect. Missing a day is not failure; it is feedback. What matters most is that you do not allow one miss to become a pattern.

The solution is simple: follow the "never miss twice" rule. If you skip one day, recommit immediately. The danger lies not in missing once but in allowing one slip to break your system.

Consistency is built on discipline, not perfection. Adjust quickly. Forgive yourself. Return to the habit the next day.

WHAT TO AVOID WHEN BUILDING HABITS

Build with simplicity, clarity, and consistency. Refine slowly. Start with one habit, not ten.

Avoid these common pitfalls when trying to build new habits:

- Trying to do too much too fast
- Making the habit too complex

- Relying on motivation instead of designing a structure
- Forgetting the link between the habit and your purpose
- Tracking too many things at once
- Failing to celebrate small wins

YOUR LIFE IS BUILT DAILY

Every goal you have, every vision you've written, every dream you've dared to believe in, it all depends on what you choose to do today.

Your habits are how your life is being built. They are either scaffolding for success or shackles of stagnation. They are not neutral; they are always working for or against your future.

You don't need to jack around with complicated plans or massive overhauls. You need small, smart habits built on structure, purpose, and discipline. Then you need to do them every single day.

This is how you build the life you were designed to live: one action, one decision, one habit at a time.

> *The secret of your future is hidden in your daily routine.*
> —Mike Murdock

12

TRACKING HABITS AS KEY PERFORMANCE INDICATORS (KPIS)

In business, Key Performance Indicators—or KPIs—are essential metrics that tell you whether the organization is making measurable progress toward its strategic goals. They provide feedback, reveal inefficiencies, identify growth, and guide decision-making. No successful enterprise functions without them.

In your personal life, **your habits are your KPIs**.

They are not just routines or rituals. They are measurable indicators of whether your daily behaviors are aligning with your Purpose, building toward your Vision, and executing your Goals. Every habit you practice consistently gives you tangible proof of whether you are compounding in the right direction or drifting off course.

Your daily habits, consistently executed over time, will determine your future.

Tracking your habits transforms intention into actionable clarity; it makes the invisible visible. Without tracking, you're making assumptions about your performance. With tracking, you're making informed decisions about your life.

WHY HABIT TRACKING IS ESSENTIAL FOR PERSONAL SUCCESS

When implemented properly, habit tracking becomes one of the most practical and powerful self-leadership tools available. It takes guesswork out of your growth and replaces it with structured, data-informed insight into how you're living each day.

Tracking habits allows you to:

STAY ACCOUNTABLE

You can't manage what you don't measure. Tracking ensures that your actions are not based on feelings, memory, or assumptions. It builds honesty with yourself and keeps your behavior in front of your eyes, where you can't ignore it.

MAKE ADJUSTMENTS QUICKLY

Patterns emerge when you track consistently. If you repeatedly miss a habit, it's a signal. Perhaps it's too complex, not properly anchored to a cue, or misaligned with your energy levels. Data replaces self-blame with a useful diagnosis.

CELEBRATE PROGRESS (EVEN WHEN RESULTS AREN'T IMMEDIATE)

Some of your most important outcomes, getting in shape—launching a business, or becoming financially independent—take months or years to realize. Tracking allows you to celebrate *process wins* in the meantime, reinforcing the behavior long before external success arrives.

BUILD MOMENTUM

Every completed habit is a vote for your future self. The more consistently you check boxes, the more confident you become. Visual progress, whether it's a calendar streak or a dashboard, builds emotional momentum and cultivates discipline.

MEASURE ALIGNMENT WITH VISION AND GOALS

Habit tracking is not just a productivity tool; it's a purpose alignment tool. It tells you if what you're doing today still supports where you said you want to go in one, three, or ten years.

FOCUS ATTENTION ON WHAT MATTERS

Your attention follows what you track. When you track your habits, you naturally spend more time and energy on what matters most and less on distractions, busywork, or reactive behavior.

Understanding the power of habits, habit stacks, and developing success strategies is key to the successful execution of your goals. Implementing these disciplines can be a struggle. It is imperative to establish your non-negotiable daily habits that you will commit to to ensure success.

DAILY HABITS—YOUR NON-NEGOTIABLES

In the Personal Success System, **non-negotiable daily habits are micro-KPIs**—small, strategic behaviors repeated every day to support long-term transformation. These are not optional or peripheral. They are the essential building blocks of your identity and momentum.

You should meet these Criteria for Daily Habits™:

1. SIMPLE ENOUGH TO DO EVEN ON YOUR WORST DAYS

Complexity is the enemy of consistency. Start with habits that are embarrassingly easy: one push-up, one budget check, or one gratitude entry. You can always build up from there, but consistency must come first.

2. ALIGNED WITH YOUR CURRENT QUARTERLY GOALS

Your habits should directly reinforce your active goals. If your Quarterly Goal is to improve health, you should build habits around movement, sleep, nutrition, reading, or networking. When the quarter changes, your habits can pivot with it.

3. SUPPORTIVE OF YOUR PHYSICAL, MENTAL, AND FINANCIAL WELL-BEING

Personal development must be sustainable. Habits that energize your body, calm your mind, and stabilize your finances create the conditions necessary for meaningful progress in all areas of life.

CORE CATEGORIES OF TRACKABLE DAILY HABITS

There are numerous high-quality books about building habits. I've learned actionable information from many of them. To avoid overwhelm and increase clarity, it is practical to categorize your habits into your core life focus areas. The PSS framework recommends tracking your habits around your 7 Fs Matrix.

DAILY AND WEEKLY HABITS: SUCCESS IN YOUR CORE LIFE FOCUS AREAS

The PSS uses the **7 Fs Matrix** to help you grow in the most essential areas of life. These are the seven domains that, when developed intentionally, create a balanced, meaningful, and purpose-driven life.

Tracking daily and weekly habits in each of these areas ensures that you don't just make progress in one lane; you grow in a way that supports your whole identity, calling, and well-being.

1. FAITH

This is the foundation of everything. Whether expressed through prayer, Scripture, devotion, or reflection, faith habits help you stay anchored in your purpose, values, and beliefs. They renew your mind and fuel your spirit.

Sample Habits

- Read a passage of scripture or a devotional.
- Meditate, pray, or journal for five minutes.
- Reflect on how your values showed up today.
- Practice gratitude intentionally.
- Listen to a faith-based podcast or teaching.

2. FITNESS

Your body is the vehicle through which your purpose is lived. Fitness habits protect your energy, discipline, and resilience. A healthy body supports a clear mind, consistent emotions, and long-term productivity.

Sample Habits

- Drink 16 ounces of water first thing each morning.
- Complete a 20-minute walk, workout, or stretch.
- Prepare or eat one whole, unprocessed meal.
- Limit or eliminate known inflammatory foods.
- Get at least seven hours of sleep and track your bedtime.

3. FAMILY

Family represents your most sacred relationships: your spouse, partner, children, or future family. These are the people you are called to love, lead, and serve with intentionality. Family habits build connection, trust, and long-term impact.

Sample Habits

- Speak words of affirmation to your spouse or child.
- Share a weekly or daily meal with no devices.
- Pray, read, or reflect together in a specific manner as a family.
- Plan one memory-making activity per week.
- Ask intentional questions and listen deeply.

4. FOCUS

This is your work, calling, business, or academic pursuit. Focus habits help you execute the work that matters most, effectively, creatively, and without burnout. These habits drive productivity and momentum toward your 1-Year and Quarterly Goals.

Sample Habits

- Identify and execute your top three priorities each morning.
- Block 60–90 minutes for deep, distraction-free work.
- Start your day before checking email or social media.
- End your workday with a review or shutdown routine.
- Track progress on current projects or tasks.

5. FINANCES

Money is not the goal, but managing it wisely enables you to live out your purpose, reduce stress, and invest in people and projects that matter. Financial habits reflect stewardship, discipline, and future-focused living.

Sample Habits

- Log your daily expenses or transactions.
- Check your budget or dashboard each evening.
- Move a small amount into savings or debt payoff.
- Meal plan or avoid one unnecessary purchase.
- Review a financial goal or metric weekly.

6. FRIENDS

Your relationships outside your home also matter. Friendships, mentors, and communities of support bring encouragement, accountability, and joy. Friendship habits build trust and connection over time, intentionally.

Sample Habits

- Text, call, or check in with a friend or mentor.
- Schedule one conversation, coffee, or connection per week.
- Send a thank-you or appreciation message.
- Invite someone into your growth or celebration.
- Engage with your community, church, or group.

7. FUN

Fun isn't just recreation; it's renewal. Fun habits protect your joy, foster creativity, and prevent burnout. They remind you that life isn't only about progress; it's also about presence, passion, and play.

Sample Habits

- Play a game, practice a hobby, or explore an interest.
- Schedule thirty minutes of "unstructured joy" time.
- Create something just for fun: music, writing, or cooking.
- Plan a trip, outing, or activity that excites you.
- Laugh with others or watch something uplifting.

HOW TO TRACK HABITS IN THE 7 FS FRAMEWORK

Use a habit tracker—digital or analog—and list one to three key behaviors under each F. Keep the list short, strategic, and realistic. The goal is to **build consistency**, not perfection.

Daily Habit Tracking Tips

- Review your tracker and Vision-Execution Snapshot first thing in the morning.
- Check off completed habits every evening.
- Adjust weekly based on what's working or stalling.
- Look for patterns, not perfection.
- Use habit streaks to build momentum and identity.

Weekly Review Prompts

- What change can I make to simplify or improve execution?

HOW TO TRACK HABITS EFFECTIVELY

To maximize the benefits of habit tracking, use a system that is visible, simple, and integrated into your daily or weekly review rhythm.

USE A VISUAL TRACKER

Choose a format that resonates with you: a printed habit grid, a mobile app, or a custom dashboard. Visual progress matters. Every completed box builds identity and self-trust; every missed one provides learning data. A simple habit tracker is included at the end of this section as one easy tool to implement.

TRACK WHAT MATTERS MOST

Don't try to track everything. Start with three to five habits that directly support your top goals or values. Once these become automatic, you can add more. Focus on impact, not volume.

REVIEW CONSISTENTLY

Pair your habit tracking with a structured **Daily Review** (5–10 minutes) and **Weekly Review** (20–30 minutes). This ensures you're not just collecting data but learning from it and optimizing your execution over time.

CELEBRATE STREAKS AND WINS

Acknowledge consistency. This might be as simple as a verbal yes when checking a box or a more formal end-of-week summary reflection. Celebrating completion builds a positive emotional association with the behavior.

USING HABIT DATA AS A FEEDBACK LOOP

Tracking turns behavior into feedback. You begin to understand your patterns, not just what works, but *why* it works. You begin to adjust proactively, rather than reactively.

With enough data, you'll begin to identify:

- Times of day when you're most consistent.
- Days of the week when habits tend to break down.
- Whether a habit is too complex and needs simplifying.
- When a habit is working but needs to be paired with a new one for greater leverage.

This is the behavior intelligence layer of the Personal Success System: using your personal data to evolve your execution and amplify your momentum.

SELF-LEADERSHIP THROUGH HABIT METRICS

Leadership begins with **leading yourself**. Leadership without accountability is just inspiration. Habit tracking is a form of self-accountability. It demonstrates maturity, integrity, and long-term thinking.

When you track your habits:

- You stop lying to yourself about your effort.

- You build credibility with yourself.
- You create a scoreboard for your discipline.
- You train your attention to look for progress.

This kind of personal measurement is not rigid or robotic; it's responsible. It's how you manage the business of your life with excellence and clarity.

> *What gets measured gets managed.*
> —Unknown

YOUR HABITS ARE YOUR LIFE'S SCOREBOARD

Your dreams are built with discipline. Your goals are realized through execution. Your vision becomes reality only if your behaviors move in the right direction consistently.

Tracking habits transforms your intentions into action and your actions into patterns. Those patterns are your personal KPIs. They tell the truth about where your life is headed. They give you the information you need to adjust, to accelerate, or to stay the course.

Managing your life is like a mission. Lead your future like a leader. Track your habits like your dreams depend on it, because they do.

DISCIPLINE IS THE ENGINE

> *Motivation gets you started. Discipline keeps you going.*
> —Jim Rohn

You don't rise to the level of your dreams. You rise to the level of your disciplines.

The PSS gives you the structure. Your vision gives you inspiration, but your daily and weekly habits are the engine.

The people who succeed aren't the ones who do everything perfectly. They're the ones who do the right things consistently, imperfectly, and relentlessly.

So if you're serious about quitting the cycle of jacking around, get serious about your daily and weekly execution. That's where transformation lives. That's where lives are built.

WILMA RUDOLPH—FROM CRIPPLED CHILD TO OLYMPIC CHAMPION

One of the most compelling and instructive stories of goal setting, perseverance, and purpose alignment is that of Wilma Rudolph, a woman who overcame staggering odds to become a global icon of resilience and excellence.

HUMBLE BEGINNINGS AND OVERWHELMING CHALLENGES

Born on June 23, 1940, in the segregated town of Clarksville, Tennessee, Wilma was the twentieth of 22 children in a deeply impoverished African American family.[100] Her father worked as a railroad porter, and her mother as a maid. Their resources were limited, and access to quality medical care was almost nonexistent, especially for Black children in the segregated South.[101]

Weighing only 4.5 pounds at birth and born prematurely, Wilma's life began in fragility.[102] As a child, she was frequently sick with illnesses ranging from pneumonia to scarlet fever. At the age of four, it was polio that dealt her the most devastating blow, leaving her with a weakened left leg and foot, twisted and partially paralyzed.[103]

At the time, polio had no cure, and her prognosis was grim. Doctors told her family that she would never walk again without the aid of leg braces.[104] Most would have accepted that fate. Wilma, even as a young child, did not.

A VISION BORN FROM PAIN

From the earliest days, Wilma Rudolph had a vision not just to walk again, but to run—and become the fastest woman in the world.[105]

This was more than a dream; it was a clear, personal vision that would shape the next two decades of her life. It wasn't rooted in ego or external success but born from a deeply personal purpose: to prove that adversity could be overcome, that no diagnosis or circumstance could define her, and that her life would be bigger than her limitations.

Her values, forged in hardship, became her internal compass: perseverance, faith, courage, family loyalty, and quiet determination.

Her mother, Blanche Rudolph, was her greatest champion. They would travel over fifty miles round-trip each week to Nashville so Wilma could receive therapy at Meharry Medical College, one of the few places that treated Black patients.[106] At home, Blanche massaged Wilma's leg four times a day, just as the doctors instructed.[107] This routine went on for years.

SETTING MICRO-GOALS AND CELEBRATING MILESTONES

Wilma's first goal was simple but revolutionary for her situation: to walk with a brace. When that was achieved, her next goal was to walk without it. Then came her first unassisted step, then a full lap around her yard.

By the time she was nine years old, she had defied the odds and walked without support, a miracle by every medical standard of the day.[108] She wasn't done. With each milestone, her vision expanded.

By age twelve, she decided to run competitively. She joined her junior high basketball team, even though she was initially clumsy and uncoordinated.[109] Her goal was to become agile, athletic, and explosive.

In high school, her athleticism caught the eye of Ed Temple, the head track coach at Tennessee State University. He immediately saw potential and discipline in Wilma, despite her lack of formal training.[110] Under his mentorship, she joined the Tigerbelles, a track club that trained high-potential athletes.

Her new 10-Year Vision became clear: becoming an Olympic champion. This was not a far-off fantasy. It was a purpose-rooted, vision-backed, goal-structured pursuit.

WILMA'S GOAL CASCADE IN ACTION

In reviewing Wilma's story, here is how I interpret her winning strategies relating to the Personal Success System's goal-setting model:

10-Year Vision
- Become the fastest woman in the world and win Olympic gold medals.

3-Year Vision
- Qualify for the US Olympic Team and compete on the world stage.

1-Year Goals
- Become the top high school sprinter in Tennessee.
- Earn a full athletic scholarship to college.
- Break state records in the 100- and 200-meter sprints.

Quarterly Goals
- Improve time in the 100-meter dash by 0.2 seconds.
- Increase training volume and incorporate strength drills.
- Win three regional competitions.
- Study tape of elite runners to refine technique.
- Practice visualization and mental toughness routines.

Every action she took, every practice, every competition, every disciplined routine served her greater purpose. Her mother and Coach Temple both provided accountability, encouragement, and structure.

THE BREAKTHROUGH: 1956 AND 1960 OLYMPICS

At just sixteen years old, Wilma qualified for her first Olympics, the 1956 Games in Melbourne, Australia, where she earned a bronze medal as part of the 4x100 meter relay team.[111] It was a stepping stone and a wake-up call. She wasn't done.

She returned home more focused than ever. Her 3-Year Vision became a 4-Year Plan: dominate the next Olympics.

Wilma trained relentlessly. By the time the 1960 Rome Olympics arrived, she was in peak form. The world watched in awe as she won three gold medals:

- 100 meters
- 200 meters
- 4x100 meter relay

She became the first American woman in history to win three gold medals in track and field during a single Olympics.[112] [113] More than that, she became a symbol of hope, dignity, and power for women, African Americans, and people with disabilities around the world.[114]

LEGACY: PURPOSE-DRIVEN SUCCESS THAT INSPIRED GENERATIONS

Wilma didn't stop after winning. She retired from competition at twenty-two, determined to use her platform to inspire others. She became an educator, coach, and advocate for civil rights and youth sports.[115]

She said, "The triumph can't be had without the struggle."[116]

She lived that truth. Her story is proof that a clear vision, rooted in deep purpose and brought to life through structured, intentional goals, can change not just a life, but history.

WHY WILMA'S STORY MATTERS TO YOU

You may not be training for Olympic gold, but your calling is no less important. Like Wilma, you have challenges. Like Wilma, you have a vision worth chasing, and like Wilma, if your purpose is clear and your goals are aligned, nothing can stop you.

So don't let your past define your future.

- Let your Purpose ignite it.
- Let your Vision direct it.
- Let your Goals build it—one quarter, one year, one victory at a time.

WHY IMPLEMENTATION MATTERS

The PSS bridges the gap between vision and execution. By setting a JACKED Framework and establishing actionable habits, you create a sustainable process for achieving your dreams. Success is not about occasional bursts of effort; it's about consistent, intentional action over time.

In the next section, we'll focus on staying accountable and sustaining momentum, ensuring that your progress continues long after the initial excitement fades.

SECTION SUMMARY: GOAL SETTING IN THE QUIT JACKING AROUND PERSONAL SUCCESS SYSTEM

A goal properly set is halfway reached.
—Zig Ziglar

Overview: This chapter outlines the critical role of goals as the bridge between Vision and Reality. Within the Quit Jacking Around Personal Success System, goals are not standalone checklists; they are strategically aligned actions grounded in purpose (DNA) and designed to move you closer to your long-term vision.

1. GOALS – THE BRIDGE BETWEEN VISION AND REALITY

- Definition: Goals translate your long-term vision and core convictions (DNA) into concrete, measurable outcomes.
- Function: They connect who you are (Purpose and Values), where you're going (10-Year and 3-Year Vision), and what you do today (1-Year and Quarterly Goals).

2. WHY GOALS MATTER

- Direction: Clarify where to point your energy.
- Focus: Choose saying yes to priorities and no to distractions.

- Motivation: Provide a compelling *why* when challenges arise.
- Feedback: Serve as a progress scoreboard, allowing recalibration.
- Accountability: Prevent "jacking around" by giving your time, energy, and effort a clear point.

3. SCIENCE-BACKED INSIGHTS ON GOAL EXECUTION

1. **Goal-Setting Effectiveness**
   - Specific, challenging goals yield better performance than vague or easy ones.
   - Written plans correlate with about 30 percent faster growth (e.g., in business).
   - Overly difficult goals can backfire. Only about 10 percent of high-difficulty goals are achieved, risking motivation loss.

2. **Neuroscience of Goal Pursuit**
   - Success depends on both a will (motivation) and a way (cognitive strategy).
   - Executive functions (attention, working memory, inhibitory control) are crucial.
   - With repetition, brain pathways automate goal-related behaviors, shifting from effortful control to habit.

3. **Strategy Execution Challenges**
   - Poor implementation as the top cause of strategic failure.

- Common barriers include unclear responsibilities, lack of prioritized objectives, and poor communication.
- Few employees understand their organization's purpose; as a result, they lack trust in leadership's direction.

4. **Effective Execution Strategies**
    - Frameworks like PSS ensure clear, measurable goals and consistent progress tracking.
    - Models such as the Strategy Kernel (diagnose, craft policy, implement actions) improve coherence.
    - Emerging AI tools can assist with goal alignment, SMART-goal wizards, and automated progress insights.

4. THE PSS GOAL-SETTING CASCADE

1. **DNA (Purpose + Values)**
    - The unshakable foundation. Goals must resonate with your identity and guiding convictions.

2. **Vision (10-Year and 3-Year)**
    - The destination and the map. Your Vision gives context to every goal.

3. **1-Year Goals**
    - Major milestones you must accomplish this year to stay aligned with Vision.

4. **Quarterly Goals (90-Day Sprints)**
   - Break each 1-Year Goal into three to five focused outcomes per quarter to maintain urgency and clarity.

5. **Weekly Focuses**
   - Tactical priorities for each week; these build your Quarterly Goals.

6. **Daily Actions and Habits**
   - The real work: small, consistent behaviors that compound into goal achievement.

Key Principle: Missed Quarterly Goals often trace back to daily inconsistency. Consistent, small choices yield big results.

5. THE JACKED FRAMEWORK

A six-step, acronym-driven system to set powerful, aligned goals—rooted in proven principles (GROW, SMART) but delivered with Quit Jacking Around's practical, irreverent tone.

1. **J — Justify Your Goal**
   - **What** exactly do you want? **Why** does it matter?
   - Ensure it aligns with your Purpose and long-term Vision.
   - Include the "positive payoff" of success and the "cost of inaction."

2. **A — Assess Your Reality**
   - **Where** are you starting from?
   - Inventory strengths, resources, and skills.
   - Identify challenges, gaps, and limiting beliefs.
   - Ground your plan in unvarnished reality (no wishful thinking).

3. **C — Create Your Winning Plan**
   - Brainstorm multiple strategies (at least three to five).
   - Enlist support: mentors, tools, systems, partners.
   - Select the most promising approach (or combination).
   - Design milestone checkpoints that excite you and feel achievable.

4. **K — Knock Out Obstacles**
   - Anticipate external barriers (time, money) and internal barriers (fear, self-doubt).
   - For each obstacle, craft a countermeasure (e.g., schedule backup workouts, install a spending freeze app).
   - Identify limiting beliefs and replace them with empowering truths.
   - Build resilience into your plan so when "life throws a punch," you punch back.

5. **E — Execute with Excellence**
   - Break your plan into **specific tasks** and assign **deadlines** (weekly, monthly).

- Write each step in SMAART language:
  - **S**pecific
  - **M**easurable
  - **A**ttainable (yet aspirational)
  - **A**ligned (with Purpose/Vision)
  - **R**elevant
  - **T**ime-bound
- Use simple action-plan tables or lists (Tool templates provided).
- Take the first step immediately—momentum fuels motivation.

6. **D — Drive It Home (Dedicate and Deliver)**
   - Revisit your compelling *why* regularly; visualize the payoff and the cost of inaction.
   - Track progress with KPIs, habit trackers, or weekly accountability meetings with yourself or a partner.
   - Celebrate every milestone (e.g., small rewards at each $1,000 saved).
   - Analyze setbacks dispassionately; adjust tactics instead of quitting.
   - Rinse and repeat: maintain unwavering commitment until the goal is achieved.

6. THE POWER OF QUARTERLY GOALS

- **Purpose**: A 90-day horizon is long enough for meaningful progress yet short enough to maintain focus and urgency.

- **Process**: Each quarter becomes a sprint aligned with your 1-Year Goals.
- **Review Questions**:
    1. What progress did I make?
    2. What did I learn?
    3. What adjustments are needed next quarter?
- **Benefit**: Builds consistency, agility, and confidence. Quarterly Wins fuel momentum for the next quarter.

7. CLARIFYING QUARTERLY GOALS WITH JACKED

1. **Justify**: Write a vivid 90-day goal statement (e.g., "Save $5,000 by Mar 31"). Include the benefits and risks of inaction.
2. **Assess**: Review last quarter's data; list strengths (e.g., extra income sources) and obstacles (e.g., impulse spending).
3. **Create**: Brainstorm three to five strategies (e.g., cancel subscriptions, meal prep, pick up freelance gigs). Choose a combined approach.
4. **Knock Out**: Identify barriers (e.g., weekend social eating) and plan countermeasures (e.g., limit eating out to one meal per week). Replace limiting beliefs ("I never stick to budgets") with empowering truths ("I am the boss of my money").
5. **Execute**:
    - **Milestones**: Save $1,250 per month.
    - **Weekly Actions**: Cancel subscriptions by January 10; meal prep Sundays; secure first freelance gig by January 20.
    - **KPI**: Track weekly net savings in a spreadsheet.

- o **Resources**: Budget app; friend accountability; meal-planning templates.
- o **Immediate Next Step**: Set up a budget tracker on January 1; cancel the first unwanted subscription.

6. **Drive**: Weekly Friday check-ins, $1,000 reward "mini-treat," adapt tactics if KPI slips. Revisit your "why" (e.g., peace of mind, investment readiness) when motivation wanes.

Pro Tip: When you write your Justify statement, start with the deadline and work backward. This keeps the finish line clearly in view.

8. STATING GOALS IN A POSITIVE TENSE

- **Neuroscience and Psychology**:
    - o Positive affirmations activate reward centers (ventral striatum, VMPFC), promoting neuroplasticity and emotional resilience.
    - o Affirmations reduce stress responses and strengthen self-esteem via self-affirmation theory.
    - o Positive framing helps filter distractions and sustain focus (similar to sports psychology research).

- **Practical Guidelines**:
    1. Use the present tense ("I am a disciplined saver" rather than "I will be").

2. Make statements specific and emotionally charged.
3. Repeat consistently—especially in challenging moments—to reinforce neural pathways.
4. Pair with visualization for maximum effect.

9. FROM VISION TO ACTION: THE FLOW OF EXECUTION

Purpose and Values ground every goal in who you are.

10-Year Vision paints the big-picture destination.

3-Year Vision sharpens the pathway.

1-Year Goals define the year's major milestones.

Quarterly Goals break the year into four focused sprints.

Weekly Focuses translate quarter goals into tactical weekly outcomes.

Daily Actions and Habits execute small, consistent behaviors that compound into results.

Missed quarterly targets often trace back to inconsistent daily habits. Consistent daily action is the engine of long-term success.

10. GOALS ARE MILESTONES, NOT FINISH LINES

- **Philosophy**: Goals mark progress, not endpoints. Once you reach a milestone, celebrate and immediately set the next one.
- **Habits as Compass**: Daily and weekly habits (journaling, KPI reviews, family dinners) act as compasses, keeping you pointed toward your next milestone.

- **Recalibrate and Reset**: After each milestone, conduct a brief assessment—celebrate wins, learn lessons, then set the next goal. Over time, this cycle becomes second nature.

11. WHY IMPLEMENTATION MATTERS

Setting goals without a robust execution system is a "nice idea" that usually fizzles.

The PSS bridges Vision to Reality through:

1. JACKED (Justify → Assess → Create → Knock out → Execute → Drive)
2. Quarterly Sprints for sustained urgency
3. Daily Habits that form the compound interest of success
4. Habit Tracking and Weekly Reviews to keep you honest and adaptable

Ultimate Message: Success arises from consistent, intentional action over time. Goals fuel forward motion; habits are the engine; accountability ensures you stay the course.

PART 5

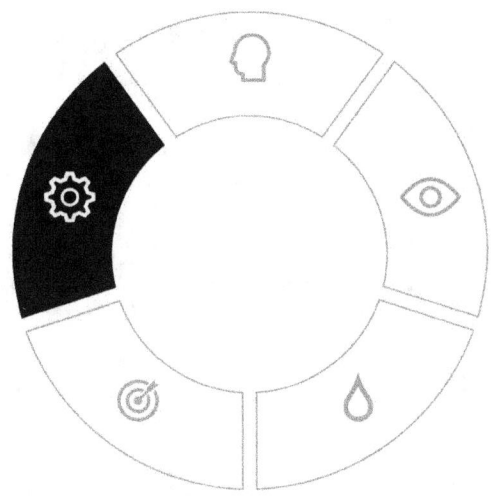

EXECUTION

Execution is the discipline of taking consistent, intentional action. It turns ideas into momentum and momentum into measurable progress. When you commit to execution, you stop waiting for perfect conditions and start creating meaningful results every single day.

13

EXECUTION: SUSTAINING MOMENTUM AND STAYING ACCOUNTABLE

Dreaming big without executing is just jacking around. Real success happens when daily action matches bold vision. Quit waiting—start executing.

Most people don't fail because they lack dreams. They fail because they lack execution. Ideas are cheap. Vision boards are easy. Inspiration fades. But day after day, brick by brick, doing the right things in the right order—that's what builds the life you say you want.

Execution is the unglamorous, relentless discipline of moving your feet when it would be easier to sit still. It's showing up when nobody's watching, pushing forward when nobody's cheering, and staying committed long after the initial excitement has worn off. It's the bridge between who you are today and who you've committed to becoming.

And here's the truth: you can't delegate execution. You can outsource tasks, hire help, and automate processes—but the discipline of doing the things that matter most? That responsibility belongs to you.

WHY EXECUTION IS THE DIFFERENCE-MAKER

The graveyard of big dreams is full of people who *almost* made it—people who got excited, started strong, and fizzled out. They thought motivation would carry them. But motivation is like the weather—it changes daily. Execution is more like your heartbeat; it has to be steady, consistent, and reliable.

Execution is not a single action; it's a rhythm. It's not about doing everything perfectly; it's about doing the right things consistently. In the PSS, execution is where your *Mindset, DNA (Purpose + Values), Vision,* and *Goals* come together in the real world. Without execution, they're just well-written intentions.

This is where you stop talking about what you're going to do someday and start building it *today*.

THE MOMENTUM PROBLEM

Getting started is hard. But staying in motion? That's the real challenge. Life will throw distractions at you. Resistance will whisper that you can skip just this one week. What's urgent will crowd out what's important. Without intentional rhythms to guide you, you will drift.

Momentum is built in small, repeated wins, not in occasional heroic efforts. You don't need one perfect week; you need a hundred good ones. You don't need to *find* time; you need to *make* time and guard it fiercely. That's why the PSS doesn't just give you big-picture clarity; it gives you the *daily, weekly, quarterly,* and *annual structures* to keep your momentum alive.

ACCOUNTABILITY: THE FUEL FOR CONSISTENCY

Even the most disciplined people are more consistent when they're accountable to someone or something outside themselves. In this chapter, you'll see how to build accountability into your execution process—not as a punishment, but as a source of fuel, clarity, and course correction. Because if you're only answering to yourself, it's too easy to let yourself off the hook.

The execution phase is where we cut through excuses, distractions, and procrastination. We trade "I'll get to it" for "It's on the calendar." We replace "I hope this works" with "Here's the system that ensures it will."

And that's the invitation of this chapter: to stop drifting, stop reacting, and start running your days like a leader—on purpose, with purpose.

You've already built the foundation:

- Your *mindset* is tuned for growth and abundance.
- Your *DNA*—your unique purpose and values—is clear.
- Your *vision* for the next 1, 3, and 10 years is defined.
- Your *goals* are mapped.

Now comes the part that separates the doers from the talkers. The next pages will walk you through how to sustain momentum, stay accountable, and live out your plan every single day—so a year from now, you're not still *talking* about your dreams . . . you're *living* them.

So, take a deep breath. Get ready to roll up your sleeves. And as always—quit jacking around. Let's execute.

THE POWER OF RHYTHMS

Success doesn't come from random hustle; it comes from intentional rhythms. Just like the body functions best with a steady heartbeat and regular breathing, your goals need consistent check-ins and recalibrations to stay alive and aligned. That's where review and planning rhythms become the backbone of execution.

The Personal Success System uses daily, weekly, quarterly, and annual rhythms to keep your habits aligned with your long-term vision. Your daily actions are fueled by your weekly focus. Your weekly focus is guided by your quarterly targets. Your quarterly targets are shaped by your annual and life-long vision. These review and planning sessions act like a GPS recalculation; they help you notice when you're off-course and correct quickly before too much time is lost. Without these rhythms, even the best habits can drift. With them, every habit becomes a building block toward something bigger.

Let the rhythm carry your momentum forward—even when life throws distractions your way.

Your PSS Rhythms:

> ➤ *The Annual Review:* One time per year, you will conduct a deep review of your PSS to measure progress, evaluate

its effectiveness, revisit its continued alignment with your Vision and DNA, and adjust.
- ➤ *The Quarterly Review:* Each quarter to reconnect, refocus, and recalibrate on your PSS, long-term goals, and actions needed to succeed.
- ➤ *The Weekly Review:* Prior to beginning a new week, you'll reflect, refocus, and realign on your daily and weekly habits and actions. Measuring their progress, effectiveness, and alignment with your quarterly goals.
- ➤ *The Daily Planning Session:* Being intentional each day to effectively execute your daily habits and actions being disciplined in moving closer to your goals each day.

THE ANNUAL REVIEW: RECONNECT, REFLECT, REALIGN

Reflection is what turns experience into real growth.

In the rush of life and the grind of goal setting, it's easy to keep moving forward without ever stopping to ask, *"Is this working? Am I still aligned with who I want to become?"*

That's the purpose of the Annual Review—an intentional pause to reflect, refocus, and realign.

Where the Quarterly Review is tactical—checking in on habits, systems, and goals—the **Annual Review is strategic and soul-level**. It's about stepping outside the noise to get a bird's eye view of your life.

THE ANNUAL REVIEW

Often, people spend more time planning a vacation than planning their year. That's why the Annual Review is so powerful: It gives you the space to think deeply about what matters most—your mindset, your legacy, your growth, and your vision. It sets the tone for your next twelve months of execution and expansion.

WHEN AND HOW TO DO IT

The future you live in is built by the structure you follow.

- **WHEN**: Schedule it at the end of the year or the very beginning of the next (December or early January). Make it non-negotiable.
- **DURATION**: Block **one to two full days**—yes, days. This is your personal strategy retreat.
- **LOCATION**: Get away from the normal. Book a cabin, a hotel, or an Airbnb. Go somewhere peaceful and inspiring. Leave the distractions behind.
- **TOOLS**: Bring a journal, your past year's planner or digital tracker, your previous Annual Review if you've done one, and this book.

THE STRUCTURE OF A PERSONAL ANNUAL REVIEW

1. RESET YOUR MINDSET: BEFORE SETTING GOALS, ASSESS YOUR INNER WORLD.

> The *external results* you create are shaped by the *internal beliefs* you hold.

Ask yourself:

- What limiting beliefs did I confront or overcome this year?
- What new beliefs or truths am I stepping into?
- Where did fear, shame, or doubt hold me back?
- Where did courage, faith, or boldness show up?

Write freely. Be honest. Use this reflection to recalibrate your mindset before setting a new direction.

2. THE LIFETIME VISUALIZER: REVISIT YOUR LEGACY

This exercise, inspired by Stephen Covey's "Begin with the end in mind," helps you reconnect to your ultimate purpose.

Review, Reflect, and Revise—Examine the 7 Fs Matrix and Lifetime Visualizers to inform yourself of progress or lack thereof on living out the life-long desired outcomes of your key priorities in life. Ask yourself:

- Where am I off track in each life focus area?
- Where am I on track?
- What specific changes do I need to make in a particular area?
- Which of these changes should be a priority in the next year and quarter?

3. REVIEW YOUR VISION-EXECUTION SNAPSHOT

(10- and 3-Year Visions and 1-Year Goals)

Pull out your current 10-Year, 3-Year, and 1-Year Visions. Reread them slowly.

Then reflect:

> - 10-Year Vision: Is this still the future I want? Am I on the path to becoming that person?
> - 3-Year Vision: Am I building the systems, habits, and relationships that will make this future possible?
> - 1-Year Goals: Did I live aligned with this in the last 12 months? What progress was made?

Update any part of your vision that feels outdated, unclear, or uninspiring. The Annual Review is your permission slip to evolve.

4. REFLECT ON THE PAST YEAR

Use these prompts to review the last twelve months with depth and intentionality:

What Went Well?

- What goals did I accomplish?
- What habits did I build?
- What relationships were strengthened?
- What breakthroughs or wins am I most proud of?

What Didn't Go Well?

- Where did I fall short?
- What goals or habits did I abandon—and why?
- What systems, people, or mindsets held me back?
- Where did I waste time, energy, or resources?

What Did I Learn?

- What lessons emerged from success?
- What lessons emerged from failure?
- How did I grow emotionally, spiritually, mentally, or physically?

Take time with this. Re-read journal entries, planners, or notes from the year. Look at your digital photos or calendar to jog your memory. Pattern recognition is key—spotting what worked and what didn't is how you course-correct.

5. REFLECT ON THE PAST QUARTER

Zoom in on the final ninety days:

- What momentum did I build or lose?
- Which habits became sustainable? Which fell apart?
- What feedback did I receive (from people or results)?
- What needs to be fixed or reinforced heading into the new year?

This quarterly reflection sharpens your ability to forecast and set up your next quarter for success.

6. DESIGN THE YEAR AHEAD

Using everything you've uncovered:

- Set three to five Annual Goals that align with your vision and priorities.
- Break them down into quarterly milestones.
- Identify the core habits and systems needed to support them.
- Map out your Quarter 1 Plan: specific targets, projects, and routines.
- Update your Vision-Execution Snapshot

You may want to use:

- A fresh planner
- A digital dashboard in Notion or Trello
- A Quarterly Goal Sheet and JACKED Framework Tool

ANNUAL REVIEW SAMPLE FLOW (DAY-BY-DAY)

Don't just plan your year. Engineer it.

DAY 1: REFLECTION AND RECONNECTION

- Mindset Reset
- Lifetime Visualizer
- Review your 10-, 3-, and 1-Year Visions
- Year in Review (What went well/didn't/lessons learned)
- Emotional/spiritual check-in

DAY 2: REALIGNMENT AND PLANNING

- Q4 Review
- Set Annual Goals
- Break down into Q1 Goals
- Design strategic habits and systems
- Update your Vision-Execution Snapshot
- Schedule next quarterly reviews and accountability structures

CREATE YOUR ANNUAL SUCCESS PLAYBOOK

As you go through your Annual Review, document everything. Create a one-page Success Playbook that includes:

- Updated Vision Statements
- Key lessons from the past year
- Three to five annual goals
- Core habits and focus areas
- Q1 Goals and milestones
- Update your Vision-Execution Snapshot
- Accountability plan (coach, partner, group, etc.)

This becomes your North Star for the year. Revisit it every quarter, every month, and every time you feel lost.

DON'T JUST LIVE ANOTHER YEAR—LIVE INTENTIONALLY

The Annual Review is your chance to stop drifting and start designing. To step away from the noise and step into clarity.

Most people sleepwalk through the years and wonder why nothing changes.

You're not most people.

You are building a life of purpose, on purpose.

So, get away. Reflect deeply. Reset your direction. And then . . .

Quit jacking around—and build your best year yet.

Your annual planning and review will inform your quarters for the upcoming year. However, as outlined earlier in this book, annual goals don't succeed. So you need a planning session each quarter to review, reflect, and adjust each quarter.

Scan to Download the Annual Review Checklist and Playbook™

QUARTERLY REVIEW AND PLANNING: RECONNECT, REFOCUS, RECALIBRATE

Every ninety days, it's time to step out of the whirlwind of doing and zoom out to the big picture. Your quarterly review is the *cornerstone* of sustainable execution. It's your personal board meeting—a time to pause, reflect, and re-align with your *DNA, Vision,* and *Goals*. The quarterly review is really a similar but slightly more abbreviated version of the Annual Review.

SCHEDULE THIS LIKE A CEO:

Book at least half a day at the end of each quarter for this review. Make it sacred, no interruptions. Bring a journal, your progress tracking tools, your planner, and a quiet space. One to two days are more ideal for this practice, but that isn't an option for everyone.

THE QUARTERLY REVIEW FLOW

1. RECONNECT WITH YOUR DNA

- Review your Vision-Execution Snapshot
    - Revisit your **Purpose Statement**: Why are you doing what you're doing?
    - Review your **Core Values**: Are you living in alignment with what matters most?
- Reaffirm your **Identity Beliefs**: Are you thinking and acting like the kind of person who achieves your vision?

2. REVISIT YOUR LIFETIME VISUALIZER, 7 FS MATRIX, 10-YEAR AND 3-YEAR VISION

- Contemplate your lifetime desired outcomes across your life priorities.
- Remind and reimagine where you want to be 10 years from now. Then imagine how you want to show up three years from today.
- Ask: *Am I on the trajectory to that future?*
- Identify any course corrections. What needs to change now to keep you aligned with that future?

3. EVALUATE THE 1-YEAR GOALS

- Review progress on your annual goals. Are they still aligned with your vision?
- For each goal:
    - Did I hit the target?
    - What worked well?
    - What didn't work, and why?
    - What lessons am I taking forward?

4. SET NEW QUARTERLY GOALS

- Based on your vision and one-year goals, what three to five Quarterly Targets should you set for the next ninety days?
- Break these down into Monthly Milestones.
- For each goal, clarify:
    - The desired outcome

        - The lead indicators (habits, inputs)
        - How you'll measure success
   - Complete the JACKED Framework for the goal

5. UPDATE SYSTEMS AND HABITS

- What weekly or daily habits need to change or be added?
- Which tools or trackers do you need to update?
- Update your Vision-Execution Snapshot
- Who can hold you accountable?

Quarterly planning ensures that your daily actions are always connected to your ultimate vision. Once you have your quarter review and planning session done, it is important to establish the weekly routines, habits, and actions you will execute to accomplish your desired outcomes.

Scan to Download the Quarterly Review Plan and Checklist™

THE WEEKLY REVIEW: REFLECT, REFOCUS, REALIGN

Don't just work through a list; structure your time around what matters most.

The **Weekly Review** is the heartbeat of sustained execution in the Personal Success System. It is where clarity is restored, momentum is recaptured, and your compass is recalibrated. Without it, even the best plans drift. With it, you become unstoppable.

The Weekly Review isn't just a planning session; it's a *strategic ritual* that transforms experience into insight, and intention into execution. It helps you step out of the whirlwind of the past week and prepare to lead yourself with purpose into the next.

WHEN TO DO IT

- Frequency: Once per week—non-negotiable.
- Time: thirty to ninety minutes, depending on depth.
- Best Days: Friday afternoon (to close the week) or Sunday (to prepare for the week ahead).
- **Location:** Quiet space, away from distractions. Coffee shop, home office, or a dedicated corner for reflection.
- **Tools:** Your Vision-Execution Snapshot, calendar, journal or tracking tools, and Weekly Review template or checklist.

EXPANDED WEEKLY REVIEW FLOW

1. REVIEW QUARTERLY GOALS AND LONG-TERM VISION IN YOUR VISION-EXECUTION SNAPSHOT

Start by zooming out. Reconnect with your current Quarterly Goals and, when needed, revisit your 1-Year, 3-Year, and 10-Year Visions.

Ask:

- What did I do this week that moved me closer to my quarterly outcomes?
- Which priority goals were neglected, and why?
- Is my weekly behavior aligned with my long-term identity and aspirations?

This keeps the big picture front and center so you don't get lost in busywork.

People often sacrifice what matters most on the altar of the urgent. The Weekly Review prevents that.

2. CELEBRATE WEEKLY WINS AND PROGRESS

Take time to *celebrate progress*, no matter how small. You're reinforcing behavior by affirming it.

Write down:

- Three wins (big or small) from the week.
- One specific moment you showed up with excellence, discipline, or courage.

- Progress made on any habits, goals, or systems.

This cultivates gratitude, builds motivation, and reinforces your identity as someone who follows through.

Pro Tip: Keep a **Wins Journal** to track these weekly. Review it quarterly and annually for a confidence boost and gratitude anchor.

3. IDENTIFY OBSTACLES, BOTTLENECKS, AND RESISTANCE

Growth only comes when you're honest with yourself. Use the Weekly Review to analyze what *didn't* work.

Ask:

- What goals or habits did I miss—and why?
- What distractions or interruptions derailed me?
- What internal resistance (fear, procrastination, perfectionism) showed up?
- Where did I waste time, energy, or focus?

This isn't about guilt; it's about *data*. When you understand where the friction is, you can design systems to eliminate it.

4. ADJUST PRIORITIES BASED ON INSIGHT

Once you've identified gaps and friction, it's time to **refine your plan**.

- What's still important this coming week?
- What needs to be delegated, postponed, or deleted?

- What shifted in your life that requires a pivot in priorities?
- Are you operating from vision—or reacting to urgency?

The goal is not to do everything; it's to do the *right things* consistently. Refine your Top Three Weekly Priorities to reflect your deepest goals.

5. SCHEDULE TIME BLOCKS FOR EXECUTION

Now that you've clarified what matters, **put it in the calendar**.

- Schedule Deep Work Blocks for your most meaningful goals.
- Add Admin Blocks to handle routine tasks.
- Include Recovery Blocks to maintain your physical and emotional energy.
- Block Goal Time for anything that builds your future (like writing, product development, fitness, learning).

Without this, your priorities are just intentions. Time blocking turns intentions into commitments.

Pro Tip: Use **color-coding** to see at a glance where your time is going. Ask: *Does my calendar reflect my vision?*

6. REFLECT ON PERSONAL SYSTEMS AND HABITS

Your systems drive your behavior. Your habits shape your identity. Each week, review:

- Which habits did I follow through on?
- Which ones broke down?

- What small tweaks could improve consistency?
- Are my routines still aligned with my energy and goals?

Update or optimize:

- Morning and evening routines
- Health and fitness practices
- Digital organization
- Task management systems

Remember: Systems should *serve* you, not enslave you.

7. REVIEW KEY METRICS AND TRACKERS

Look at the data:

- Habit tracker completion percentages
- Goal progress scorecards
- Streak charts
- Budget, nutrition, exercise, or other performance indicators

Ask:

- What trends are emerging?
- What metrics improved or declined—and why?
- What's one number I want to improve next week?

This keeps your decisions data-driven, not emotion-driven.

8. REVISIT WEEKLY ROLES AND RESPONSIBILITIES

PSS encourages you to live intentionally in all areas of life. Reflect on how you showed up in your core roles:

- As a leader or entrepreneur
- As a spouse or parent
- As a friend or community member
- As a steward of your health, finances, or faith

Ask:

- Where was I aligned with my values?
- Where did I fall short?
- What can I do differently next week in each role?

This adds depth to your weekly reflection and keeps your life balanced and meaningful—not just productive.

9. CAPTURE IDEAS AND LOOSE ENDS

Every week brings inspiration, ideas, and unfinished tasks. Before the week ends:

- Capture stray thoughts or ideas in your journal or digital system.
- List incomplete tasks for review or scheduling.
- Archive or declutter any unneeded items from your inbox, notes, or workspace.

This "brain drain" clears mental clutter so you can start the next week fresh and focused.

10. RENEW YOUR MINDSET AND MOTIVATION

Close your Weekly Review by checking in with your **mindset** and **heart**.

- Reaffirm your identity: *Who am I becoming?*
- Revisit your purpose, Lifetime Visualizer, or affirmations.
- Write a note to your future self.
- Visualize yourself succeeding next week.

Ask:

- What kind of energy do I want to bring into the week?
- What virtues or character traits do I want to embody?

This isn't fluff; it's fuel. You lead best when you're connected to purpose.

WEEKLY REVIEW TEMPLATE (SAMPLE PROMPTS)

Here's a sample you can customize:

- Top Three Weekly Wins
- One Thing I'm Proud Of
- One Thing That Frustrated Me
- What Got in the Way?
- What Did I Learn?
- What Will I Do Differently Next Week?
- Top Three Priorities for Next Week
- Weekly Role Check-In
- Weekly Habit Review (scorecard percent)

- Time Blocks for Top Priorities
- Mindset and Motivation Score (1–10)
- Affirmation or Visual for the Week Ahead

A KEYSTONE HABIT FOR PEAK PERFORMANCE

The Weekly Review is a **keystone habit**—a single practice that multiplies every other habit and goal in your life. It:

- Provides clarity
- Prevents drift
- Reveals blind spots
- Strengthens consistency
- Restores purpose
- Fuels momentum

If you skip it, you slowly drift. If you commit to it, you build week-over-week growth that transforms your year.

So don't treat your Weekly Review like an optional to-do. Treat it like a *sacred space*—your personal leadership meeting. You owe it to your future self.

Set the time. Light a candle. Pour some coffee. And quit jacking around.

Your best week is waiting.

While your weekly planning and execution tactics are key to success, it is key to review, reflect, and revise with a daily review and planning habit.

Scan to Download the Weekly Review Plan and Checklist™

DAILY PLANNING SYSTEM: TURN VISION INTO ACTION

Daily planning is the execution engine of the PSS. It's where your long-term vision meets the reality of your day. While your annual and quarterly reviews set direction, your **daily plan is where traction happens**. It creates a rhythm of clarity, focus, and control that positions you for consistent progress, regardless of external circumstances.

By committing to a short daily planning session—ideally every morning or the night before—you set yourself up to win the day with intention instead of reaction.

Use these three foundational prompts to plan your day:

1. **What are the three most important things I must do today?**

    These are not just tasks; they are *your top three priorities* that directly advance your quarterly goals or key focus areas. Think of them as your non-negotiables. If everything else falls through, getting these three done still makes it a productive day.

2. **What time blocks will I use to protect my focus?**

    Priorities don't matter if they're not protected. This step ensures your top three are scheduled, not just hoped for. You assign actual blocks of time to your most meaningful work, which removes ambiguity and builds discipline.

3. **How will I stay aligned with my purpose?**

    Here, you reconnect with your DNA—your purpose, values, and long-term vision. This alignment fuels intrinsic motivation and prevents drift. You might reread your 1-Year Goal, revisit your Lifetime Visualizer, or simply review your "why" before launching into the day.

Over time, this habit trains your mind to operate from clarity rather than chaos. The result is exponential. A week of top threes equals fifteen high-value actions. One month equals sixty. A year totals over seven hundred; that's the power of daily intentionality.

Scan to Download the Daily Review Plan and Checklist™

14

EXECUTION STRATEGIES AND TOOLS: MAKE HABITS AUTOMATIC AND UNSTOPPABLE

You can have the clearest vision in the world, the most inspiring Purpose Statement, and a set of perfectly crafted goals—but without execution, they're nothing more than wishful thinking. Dreams don't build themselves. Ideas don't turn into impact by accident. The bridge between "what could be" and "what is" is paved with consistent, deliberate action.

In the Personal Success System, execution isn't an afterthought—it's the heartbeat. It's where your purpose, vision, and goals stop living on paper and start shaping your actual life. But here's the truth most people don't want to admit: execution is hard, not because we don't know what to do, but because we don't have systems that make doing it easy and sustainable.

Willpower alone is a terrible execution strategy. Motivation is inconsistent. Life is unpredictable. If you rely on "feeling ready" or "waiting for the perfect time," you'll keep circling the runway instead of taking off. That's why the PSS approach to execution focuses on building rhythms, routines, and tools that take as much decision-making out of the equation as possible. The less you have to think about whether or when to act, the more you'll actually follow through.

This chapter is your execution toolkit. You'll learn how to:

- **Stack habits** so that your wins piggyback on routines you already have.
- **Block time,** so that what matters most actually gets the space it deserves in your calendar.
- **Design morning and evening routines** that act like launchpads and landing strips for your day.
- **Manage your energy,** not just your time, so that you can do the right work at the right time for your brain and body.
- **Track your progress,** so you can see results, course-correct faster, and keep your momentum alive.

Along the way, you'll discover how to set up your environment, cues, and daily flow so execution becomes less about trying harder and more about making it nearly impossible not to follow through. You'll see that small, consistent actions—stacked and repeated—compound into massive results over time.

By the end of this chapter, you won't just have a list of productivity tips. You'll have a personal execution framework—a set of repeatable systems that align your daily actions with your highest priorities. And once that alignment is locked in, you'll find that progress stops being an uphill battle and starts feeling inevitable.

Execution is the great equalizer. Talent, resources, and timing matter—but disciplined follow-through beats them all. If you master execution, you can outpace people with more advantages, overcome obstacles that used to derail you, and build the life you've been envisioning in these pages.

Now, let's get to work—because clarity without execution is just daydreaming, and you didn't pick up this book to keep jacking around.

HABIT STACKING: BUILD MOMENTUM WITH MINIMAL RESISTANCE

In the PSS, habit stacking is a powerful tool to *automate execution* without relying on willpower. It uses the principle of anchoring a new behavior to an existing one, so you don't have to think about when or how to start.

This technique leverages what neuroscientists call cue-based repetition, where a familiar action (like brushing your teeth or pouring coffee) triggers the next habit in the chain. Over time, the sequence becomes automatic.

Examples in Practice:

- **After brushing my teeth in the evening → I journal three wins from the day**
  Reinforces positivity, gratitude, and self-awareness as part of your evening wind-down.
- **After making coffee → I review my top three priorities**
  Start your day focused, not distracted. This anchors you in purpose before the day begins.

- **After my workout → I read ten minutes of a book aligned with my vision**

    Reinforces your identity as a learner and leader. Leverages post-exercise alertness for growth.

Why it works:

- It reduces decision fatigue.
- It removes the need to create new cues.
- It taps into your existing routines and rhythms.

To implement effectively:

- Choose one anchor behavior already in your daily routine.
- Attach only one small habit at first.
- Track and reinforce consistency.

As you stack habits into routines, you build powerful, low-resistance systems that fuel transformation.

TIME BLOCKING: DEFEND YOUR PRIORITIES WITH PRECISION

Time blocking is one of the most critical tools in the PSS execution toolkit. It transforms your calendar from a passive reminder into a proactive roadmap. Rather than asking, *"What do I need to do today?"* you're answering, *"When exactly will I do what matters most?"*

This method turns your day into intentional blocks of focused activity. Each block has a purpose. Each purpose is aligned with your vision.

Types of Time Blocks to Use:

- **Deep Work Blocks**

    Sixty- to ninety-minute sessions for focused, uninterrupted work on your most important priorities. Ideal for content creation, strategic planning, vision casting, or solving complex problems.

- **Admin Blocks**

    Thirty- to sixty-minute segments for lower-leverage but necessary tasks like emails, scheduling, or paperwork. Batching these prevents them from invading your deep work time.

- **Recovery Blocks**

    These include meals, walks, meditation, or white space to recover cognitively. Essential for sustainability and creativity.

- **Goal Blocks**

    Dedicated time to your long-term aspirations—writing a book, working on a course, business development, and so on. These blocks ensure your vision remains alive and active in your calendar.

Best Practices:

- Protect your Deep Work Blocks in the morning when energy is highest.
- Color-code your calendar to distinguish between types of blocks.
- Evaluate your calendar weekly to ensure alignment with quarterly goals.

Time blocking doesn't restrict freedom; it *creates* it. It gives structure to your day so you can make progress without stress.

THE POWER OF A MORNING ROUTINE

Your morning routine is the launchpad for your day; in the Personal Success System, it's one of your most strategic execution tools. A strong morning rhythm doesn't just help you wake up; it anchors your identity, primes your mind, and builds momentum before the world makes its demands on you.

When you begin each day by executing your **daily non-negotiables**, you reinforce discipline and direction before distractions even begin. This could include reviewing your **vision statement, personal mantra, top three goals**, and **daily habits**. Whether it's prayer, journaling, a workout, reading, or simply sitting quietly with your coffee and your plan, these activities are more than routines—they are declarations of who you are becoming.

One of the most powerful morning anchors is movement. A morning workout—even a short one—tells your body and brain that you're in charge. It builds energy, sharpens mental clarity, and reinforces follow-through. Pair that with a review of your goals and calendar, and you're not just awake; you're *aligned.*

THE EVENING ROUTINE: PREPARE TO WIN TOMORROW

While the morning sets the tone, the evening is where momentum is **protected and prepared**. A purposeful evening routine allows you to close the day with reflection and set the stage for execution tomorrow.

In the PSS system, you put a capstone on your day's activities. Take a few minutes to review what you accomplished, whether that is updating your progress on key habits and goals or updating your budget. Then, remove friction in advance for the next day by doing those little tasks that ensure you easily follow through on your habits and actions. Finally, my personal favorite to end the day—in prayer or a quiet moment of meditation or reflection.

This same principle applies to other areas of your life. Review your top three priorities for tomorrow. Set out what you need for your first task or meeting. Do a short reflection on your wins, lessons, or emotions from the day. You're not just closing loops—you're building a **bridge from today's effort to tomorrow's momentum**.

Evening routines aren't about restriction. They're about *readiness*. When you wind down with intention, you wake up with direction. And when both bookends of your day are aligned with your vision, everything in between becomes more purposeful.

ENERGY MANAGEMENT VS. TIME MANAGEMENT

REDEFINING EXECUTION IN THE PERSONAL SUCCESS SYSTEM FOR REAL-WORLD BRAINS

Time management tells you what's on the clock. Energy management tells you what you're capable of.

For decades, time management has been the go-to strategy for productivity. Plan your day in hourly blocks, follow your calendar like the gospel, and you'll succeed. But for many people—especially those with ADHD or naturally dynamic energy rhythms—**this just doesn't work**.

You're not lazy. You're not undisciplined. You're wired differently.

The PSS teaches a better way: **Energy-Based Execution**—a framework that helps you stop wasting effort on rigid structure and start designing your schedule around when you're naturally most alert, creative, focused, or in need of rest.

WHY TIME MANAGEMENT FALLS SHORT (ESPECIALLY FOR ADHD BRAINS)

Time management assumes:

- That your energy is constant.
- That your attention is reliable.
- That every hour holds the same value.

Real life and real brains don't work that way.

Especially if you have ADHD, anxiety, or high creative output, you might experience:

- Sudden spikes of clarity and focus
- Energy crashes mid-day or post-meetings
- Hyperfocus windows where you're in a zone for hours
- Brain fog even during time-blocked deep work slots

Traditional time blocking doesn't account for this. It tells you *when* to work, not *when you're actually capable* of working well.

The solution isn't more structure; it's more flexibility aligned with your energy patterns.

WHAT IS ENERGY-BASED EXECUTION?

Energy-Based Execution is the practice of aligning your work, habits, and priorities with your **mental, physical, emotional, and spiritual energy**, not just with the clock.

It respects your:

- Cognitive cycles (when you're focused vs. scattered)
- Emotional capacity (when you feel driven vs. drained)
- Physical energy (when your body feels most active or still)
- Creative flow (when your ideas flow best)

It shifts the goal from: "How do I fit this task into my day?"
to
"When during my day am I most capable of doing this task well?"

IDENTIFY YOUR PERSONAL ENERGY PATTERNS

Track for 7 Days Using This Simple Log:

Time Block	Mental Focus (1–10)	Physical Energy (1–10)	Emotional State	Notes
Morning (6 a.m.–10 a.m.)				
Midday (10 a.m.–2 p.m.)				
Afternoon (2 p.m.–6 p.m.)				
Evening (6 p.m.–10 p.m.)				

You'll likely find:

- One or two **"peak focus" blocks**
- A natural **creative zone**
- Specific energy **crash periods**
- A **late-night** or **early-morning productivity spike**

This is your personal productivity fingerprint.

THE PSS ENERGY-BASED TIME BLOCKING MODEL™

Instead of blocking your time in hours, block it based on **energy availability**.

Sample Grid

Energy Zone	Ideal Tasks	Tools/Notes
High Focus	Deep work, problem-solving, strategic tasks	Airplane mode, no distractions, Pomodoro Technique
Low Focus	Admin, email, batching, routine tasks	Headphones, templates, checklists
Physical Energy	Exercise, errands, housework, active calls	Standing desk, walks, phone time
Emotional High	Visioning, journaling, affirmations	Music, morning routine, visual boards
Emotional Low	Recovery, solitude, nature, naps	Silence, breathwork, gentle movement
Creative Peak	Writing, designing, content creation	Flow playlists, free writing, sketch pads

Instead of a strict 9–10:30 a.m. deep work block, you might set a High Focus Block whenever your energy aligns, for example, 10 a.m. some days and 1 p.m. others.

STRATEGIC ENERGY HABITS TO BUILD YOUR DAY AROUND

For most people, there are natural times of the day when you can perform habit stack rituals. Often in the morning, at midday, and in the evening. Here are some strong examples:

MORNING RITUAL ANCHORS (MINDSET AND MOMENTUM)

- Wake at the same time
- Avoid phone use for the first thirty minutes

- Use prayer, scripture, meditation, or journaling to establish your identity and purpose
- Stack one small win immediately (e.g., make bed, hydrate, write top three)
- Review your Vision-Execution Snapshot

MIDDAY RECHARGE RITUALS

- Short walks
- Ten-minute guided breathing or nap
- Switch environments (desk → balcony → park)
- Energy snack (protein + water vs. sugar + crash)

EVENING SHUTDOWN RITUAL

- Close out your habit tracker
- Review your Vision-Execution Snapshot
- Review wins from the day
- Write tomorrow's top three priorities
- Power down screens thirty to sixty minutes before bed

These **energy rituals** restore capacity and make your execution sustainable, not exhausting.

ENERGY TACTICS (ADHD-FRIENDLY)

Managing energy in your day is crucial to the successful completion of your daily and weekly habits and actions. Here are some additional approaches to energy management that are tailor-made for brains that bounce between states of distraction, hyperfocus, and fatigue:

1. USE INITIATION RAMPS

- Do something easy and fun for three to five minutes to trigger engagement.
- Example: rewriting a header, sketching a visual, listening to a motivating clip.

2. MICRO-SPRINTS WITH IMMEDIATE REWARDS

- Use timers: 15- to 25-minute sprints followed by short breaks.
- Attach small rewards: a coffee, a YouTube break, a walk.

3. ENVIRONMENTAL ANCHORS

- Different spaces for different energy zones:
    - Desk = Deep Work
    - Couch = Creative Thinking
    - Standing = Calls

4. TASK BATCHING BY ENERGY TYPE

- Instead of grouping by project, group by energy:
    - All high-focus tasks back-to-back
    - All admin tasks during low-energy windows

ENERGY-ALIGNED DAILY PLANNING IN PSS

Here's how to adjust the **PSS Daily Execution Template**:

Morning Questions:

1. What are my top three priorities?
2. What energy will these tasks require?
3. When am I best equipped to execute them?

Planning Template Sample:

Task	Energy Needed	Best Block	Support System
Write proposal	High Focus	9:30–11:00	Noise-canceling
Client emails	Low Focus	2:00–2:45	Checklist
Go to the gym	Physical High	4:00–5:00	Playlist

HOW TO HANDLE ENERGY COLLISIONS AND LOW DAYS

Some days, your energy will betray you. That's life. Here's how to respond:

- **Downshift tasks**: Instead of writing a report, outline the headings.
- **Switch to another task**: Do admin or review work instead of creative.
- **Use external structure**: Call an accountability partner.
- **Stack wins**: Do two to three easy tasks fast to build momentum.

On low-energy days, don't try to crush it. Just protect your consistency and move the needle, even if it's just an inch.

ENERGY-AWARE WEEKLY REVIEW QUESTIONS

- When was I most productive—and what time/energy state was I in?
- What threw off my energy most often?
- What recovery habits helped me most?
- What energy pattern trends am I noticing?
- How can I rearrange next week to better support peak zones?

This kind of review turns your weekly planning into personal optimization.

THE REAL POWER OF ENERGY-BASED EXECUTION

Time can be wasted.
Tasks can be pushed.
But *energy is the true currency* of execution.

Managing your energy puts you in a position to:

- Work when it counts most.
- Design life around your strengths.
- Prevent burnout and mental clutter.
- Execute with intention rather than force.

When you learn to manage your energy, you stop jacking around—not because you're working harder, but because you're finally working smarter for how you're actually built.

So planning and executing your daily and weekly tasks is key to charting your course toward success, but tracking your daily and weekly progress is how you measure your success. This means having an effective tracking system you'll use is foundational to the success of your goals.

TRACKING SYSTEMS: MAKE PROGRESS VISIBLE AND TANGIBLE

Many have said it in many ways—what gets measured gets managed, and what gets managed, grows.

Tracking isn't about perfection; it's about *visibility* and *consistency*. It allows you to see patterns, adjust, and celebrate progress. The PSS integrates multiple tracking tools to support different types of goals and habits.

Core Tracking Tools:

- **Habit Trackers**

    Visual checklists to mark daily progress. These can be digital (Notion or mobile apps) or physical (printables or whiteboards). Seeing your streak grow builds momentum and motivation.

- **Goal Scorecards**

    Break down big goals into measurable steps. Track percentage completed or milestones hit. Scorecards bring clarity to longer-term objectives and help you avoid vague ambition.

- **Streak Charts**

    These reinforce consistency. Tracking how many days in a row you perform a habit (like exercise, journaling, or reading) taps into your desire to maintain momentum and avoid breaking the chain.

- **Reflection Journals**

    These are critical for tracking qualitative progress. Every day or week, log what's working, what's not, insights gained, your emotional state, and micro wins. This builds self-awareness and fosters learning.

Recommended Tools:

- **The Daily and Weekly Habit Tracker tool** in this book.
- **Digital:** Notion, Trello, or ClickUp for custom dashboards; Habitica or Streaks for habit gamification; Strides or Way of Life for simplicity.
- **Manual:** Daily and weekly printable trackers, whiteboards, planners, or bullet journals.
- **Hybrid:** Google Sheets or Excel if you like spreadsheet-based planning with visual graphs.

Tracking turns your goals into feedback loops. It shows you what's real, not just what you think is happening. And that truth is what empowers meaningful adjustments and growth.

EXECUTION FLOW: PUTTING IT ALL TOGETHER IN A DAILY RHYTHM

Here's how a PSS-aligned day might look when you combine the above systems:

Morning Routine
1. Wake up, hydrate
2. Read a short portion of your vision or Lifetime Visualizer
3. Review your Vision-Execution Snapshot
4. Review your top three priorities
5. Time block your deep work session
6. Habit stack: make coffee → review purpose

Midday Execution
1. Deep Work Block (one to two hours)
2. Admin Block (thirty minutes)
3. Lunch + Recovery Block (walk, pray, unplug)

Afternoon Focus
1. Goal Block (creative, strategic, or future-building task)
2. Check habit tracker + streak chart
3. Capture wins or lessons in a reflection journal

Evening Routine
1. Review the day
2. Write down three wins and one lesson
3. Review your Vision-Execution Snapshot
4. Prep the top three for tomorrow
5. Journal or visualize tomorrow's progress

This structure might seem simple, but over time it creates a compounding impact. You gain clarity. You reduce wasted time. You start becoming the person you were designed to be, not by chance, but by *choice*.

SYSTEMATIZE EXECUTION TO MULTIPLY IMPACT

Daily planning, habit stacking, time blocking, and tracking aren't just productivity tips. They are *core levers of personal transformation* in the PSS. They help you execute even when motivation fails, time is short, and life gets messy.

They ensure that every day becomes a vote for your vision.

You don't need more time; you need more clarity. You don't need a better plan; you need a better rhythm. You don't need to hustle harder; you need to execute smarter.

Start your day with intention. Build habits that support your goals. Track your wins and quit jacking around.

While you execute on your habits and actions each day, there are several rhythms you need to conduct to best achieve success. The first is your weekly review and planning session.

Scan to Download the Daily and Weekly Habit Tracker™

INSPIRATION IN ACTION: BETHANY HAMILTON—RIDING THE WAVE OF RELENTLESS EXECUTION

Bethany Hamilton's story isn't just about surviving a shark attack; it's about choosing to keep going when everything in your life changes in an instant, executing when it would've been easier to quit, and anchoring yourself in purpose and discipline when the spotlight fades and the struggle begins.

Born February 8, 1990, in Lihue, Kauai, Hawaii, Bethany was raised in a surfing family and began competing by age eight, even winning the Rell Sunn Menehune Surfing Championship and securing her first sponsorship by age nine.[117][118] Her future seemed destined for the pros—until October 31, 2003, when at age thirteen, she was attacked by a fourteen-foot tiger shark off Kauai's coast, losing her left arm just below the shoulder and nearly 60 percent of her blood.[119]

Age Thirteen: The Attack That Changed Everything

The shark latched onto her left arm as she surfed at Tunnels Beach with her friend Alana Blanchard. Alana's father applied a tourniquet, and she was rushed to the hospital in hypovolemic shock—yet amazingly, she survived.[120]

The Recovery: Execution Starts Small

Despite the trauma, Bethany returned to surfing just one month later, demonstrating incredible mental resilience.[121] She relearned how to paddle, balance, and rebuild strength using adapted techniques—including a custom surfboard handle devised by her father[122]—to accommodate her new reality.[123] [124]

Ninety Days Later: Back on the Board

Within 90 days of the attack, Bethany was competing again. By 2005, she won a national surfing championship, went pro by age 17, and continued achieving in major competitions.[125]

The Long Game: Purpose Over Pain

Beyond personal triumphs, she became a global advocate for resilience. Her autobiography, *Soul Surfer* (2004), was adapted into the 2011 film *Soul Surfer* and later the 2018 documentary *Unstoppable*.[126] She also launched the Beautifully Flawed Foundation to support young people with limb differences, creating community, retreats, and outreach events.[127] Today, she continues to inspire as a professional surfer, motivational speaker, and mother rooted in faith, purpose, and disciplined execution.[128]

Bethany's Formula for Execution

- A Clear Vision: Returning to surfing and reclaiming her life.
- Customized Systems: Adapting tools and techniques to her new reality.
- Gritty Execution: Daily discipline through setbacks, pain, and fear.
- Unshakable Purpose: Grounded in faith and mission—"Courage doesn't mean you don't get afraid. Courage means you don't let fear stop you," as Bethany said.

The Takeaway: Keep Paddling Forward

Bethany Hamilton shows that discipline can outweigh defeat, that your "why" can transcend your wound, and that execution depends not on circumstances but the decision to keep moving forward—one wave, one habit, one challenge at a time.

You don't need everything to be easy; you just need a clear path and a decision to take it.

EXECUTION IS A LIFESTYLE

Your goals are just the beginning.

Execution is how you build the future you imagine. It's the bridge from idea to impact, from vision to victory, from purpose to personal legacy.

The Execution Formula:

Clarity + Consistency + Regular Review + Robust Accountability = Sustainable Success

So now it's your turn.

Block the time.

Build the habits.

Track your progress.

Show up daily.

Reflect quarterly.

More importantly . . . **quit jacking around and follow through.**

15

ACCOUNTABILITY AND SUPPORT: SUCCESS IS A TEAM EFFORT

*Success isn't just about the process—
it's about the people who help you get there.*

THE COMPANY YOU KEEP—AND LET KEEP YOU

Jim Rohn famously observed, "You are the average of the five people you spend the most time with."[129] In other words, our daily circle—the conversations we have, the attitudes we absorb, the habits we witness—inevitably shape who we become. In the execution phase of your Personal Success System, this isn't a nice-to-know; it's a must-do.

Execution demands clarity, discipline, and momentum, and those qualities don't emerge in a vacuum. They're forged in the heat of your environment. When you consciously choose to surround yourself with people who challenge your thinking, model excellence, and hold you accountable, you turbocharge your ability to turn plans into reality. Conversely, if your closest five are stuck in complaint mode or are resistant to growth, their inertia becomes your ceiling.

Here's the pivot: It's not just about who you physically spend time with. It's about who you *allow* to influence your mindset and actions. Maybe you're in the same office as someone with a defeatist attitude, but you don't have to let their doubt infect your drive. Maybe you engage daily with negative news on social media, but you can curate feeds that inspire instead of deflate. In practice, this means:

1. **Audit Your Inputs.** List out the top five voices—people, podcasts, feeds, or even internalized beliefs—you engage with daily.
2. **Evaluate Their Impact.** Do they expand your horizons, challenge your status quo, and push you toward your goals? Or do they encourage complacency?
3. **Upgrade Relentlessly.** Seek out mentors, peers, and thought leaders who live out the qualities you want to embody. Invite their influence into your world through mastermind groups, accountability partnerships, or even books and podcasts that resonate with your vision.

Execution is about taking decisive action over and over again. By consciously choosing the five people (or perspectives) you let influence you, you create an ecosystem that nurtures your success. You're not just moving faster; you're moving smarter, fueled by a network that reflects the very best you can become.

BUILD SYSTEMS OF ACCOUNTABILITY

Accountability accelerates execution. It keeps you honest, consistent, and encouraged.

Here are some different accountability relationships and systems that will become vital to the successful completion of your long and short-term goals:

- Counselor: Trained to address past issues, help rewire your mind, and move you forward.
- Personal Coach: A trained professional who helps you maintain alignment, stretch your goals, and overcome limitations.
- Mentor: Someone who's gone ahead of you who can share their wisdom.
- Accountability Partner: Weekly check-ins to share goals, report progress, and troubleshoot roadblocks.
- Accountability/Mastermind Group: Monthly or bi-weekly group of peers pursuing big goals who challenge and support each other.
- Self-Accountability Systems:
    - Daily journaling
    - Weekly reviews
    - Visual progress charts
    - Monthly Report to Self documents

THE POWER OF ACCOUNTABILITY: THE BRIDGE BETWEEN INTENTION AND ACTION

Accountability isn't punishment; it's *empowerment*. It's the bridge that connects your best intentions with consistent action. Studies show just how powerful this is.

According to the American Society of Training and Development (ASTD), individuals are 65 percent more likely to meet a goal when they commit to another person and 95 percent more likely when they schedule ongoing check-ins.[130]

When someone else knows your goal, and you've committed to showing up and reporting progress, something shifts. You take it more seriously. You push through resistance. You keep going because someone's watching, cheering, and expecting you to follow through.

THE ACCOUNTABILITY ADVANTAGE

Meet Jerry, a mid-level manager who struggled for years to lose weight and stick to a fitness plan. He'd start strong every January but fall off by March.

Everything changed when Jerry partnered with a friend to do daily check-ins. Every morning, they texted each other their weight, food plan, and goals for the day. On tough days, they encouraged each other. After wins, they celebrated. That simple habit created a massive transformation.

Within a year, Jerry lost fifty pounds, gained confidence, and began crushing goals at work and home. *The secret wasn't a new diet; it was the accountability.*

YOUR PERSONAL SUPPORT TEAM

Let's break down the key roles that can help you turn intention into impact:

1. THE COUNSELOR: HEAL TO MOVE FORWARD

To create a bold future, sometimes you must deal with the past.

Limiting beliefs, unresolved trauma, and self-sabotage are often invisible anchors holding you back. A professional counselor is trained to help you process these blocks, shift your mindset, and release emotional weights that no longer serve you.

Counselors help you:

- Make peace with your past.
- Overcome mental and emotional roadblocks.
- Develop tools to manage anxiety, fear, or self-doubt.
- Rewire harmful beliefs about yourself or success.

You can't fully reach for the future while clinging to pain from the past.

If your momentum feels stalled or you're constantly battling internal resistance, it's time to stop jacking around and **talk to a counselor.**

2. THE COACH: CLARITY, STRATEGY, AND ACCOUNTABILITY

A coach isn't just for sports. In life, business, relationships, and health, coaches are trained professionals who help you *gain clarity, overcome obstacles,* and *take decisive action.*

Coaches ask powerful questions. They don't give you answers; they help you discover them. They listen deeply, challenge your thinking, and help you develop strategies that stick.

What a coach brings:

- Clarity of direction
- Alignment with your values and goals
- Structured accountability
- Support for refining your systems and habits
- Guidance during obstacles, transitions, or plateaus

Sometimes all you need to win is someone to help clear the fog and focus your fire.

COACHING FOR SUCCESS: SERENA WILLIAMS

Even at the peak of her career, tennis legend Serena Williams credits her coach with helping her grow, refine, and stay sharp. The coach wasn't just there to tweak her swing—but to analyze patterns, push limits, and keep her focused.

You don't need to be an elite athlete to benefit from coaching. *You just need a desire to grow and a commitment to take action.*

COACHING SERVICES AVAILABLE

As part of this system, coaching support is available to help you implement everything you've learned:

- ➤ **One-on-One Coaching:** Personalized support tailored to your journey.
- ➤ **Group Coaching:** Shared wisdom, encouragement, and momentum.
- ➤ **Accountability Check-ins:** Consistent sessions to stay on track and pivot as needed.

3. THE MENTOR OR EXPERT ADVISOR: LEARN FROM EXPERIENCE

A mentor is someone who's already traveled the path you're on. They have wisdom gained from both failure and success and are willing to share it so you can move faster and smarter.

Whether it's launching a business, improving finances, parenting, health, or relationships, there's someone out there who's *been there*. Tap into that knowledge.

What a mentor offers:

- Real-world experience
- Practical shortcuts and tools
- Encouragement and perspective
- Protection from avoidable mistakes

If you want to go fast, go alone. If you want to go far, go with someone who's been there before.

If you're trying to grow in a specific area, stop guessing; get a mentor and quit jacking around.

4. ACCOUNTABILITY PARTNER: A DAILY MIRROR

Accountability partners aren't optional; they're a powerful accelerant to your success.

An accountability partner checks in with you regularly about your goals. They care enough to tell you the truth. They call you out, lift you up, and celebrate your wins.

Qualities of a good accountability partner:

- Shared commitment to growth.
- Consistent communication (daily/weekly).
- Honest feedback and encouragement.
- Willingness to hold you to your standards.
- Clear boundaries and expectations.

Accountability isn't judgment; it's support with teeth.

Tip: Choose someone who takes their own growth seriously. Accountability is a two-way street.

5. ACCOUNTABILITY GROUPS: COLLECTIVE MOMENTUM

A strong peer group is one of the most powerful forces for growth. Masterminds, accountability groups, or growth pods—whatever the format—these are communities of people committed to rising together.

They're not just about sharing ideas. They're about *taking action together*.

Benefits of an Accountability Group:

- Shared experience and problem-solving.
- Structured goal setting and check-ins.
- Encouragement and emotional support.
- Expansion of perspective.
- Compound motivation from collective wins.

When you're part of the right circle, success becomes contagious.

Join or build your own mastermind. Surround yourself with doers.

6. EXECUTIVE ASSISTANTS (EA): YOUR SECRET WEAPON

Behind every high achiever is a powerhouse assistant.

My executive assistant is a non-negotiable tool to any success I achieve today. She helps keep me organized and on task and serves as a built-in accountability partner. She is tasked with ensuring I complete my key personal routines, such as working out and my other daily habits, and keeping me focused on my key business habits and activities.

Whether it's a full-time EA, a remote assistant, or a digital workflow, delegation creates space for *you* to focus on what matters most.

An EA is more than helpful; they're a *strategic asset*. They take tasks off your plate, streamline communication, schedule your priorities, and help you stay organized and on mission.

Benefits of an Executive Assistant:

- Free up time for high-impact work.
- Increase follow-through on tasks and commitments.
- Prevent burnout by offloading details.
- Maintain momentum and visibility of your goals.

If you don't have time to execute, it's time to delegate.

Can't afford a human assistant yet? Use tools like:

- **AI (like ChatGPT)** for writing, brainstorming, and planning.
- **Automation Tools** like IFTTT or Zapier to streamline workflows.
- **Scheduling Tools** like Calendly or Motion.
- **Task Managers** like Notion, ClickUp, or Todoist.

Until you can hire one, build one with systems. Don't try to do it all alone.

THE CIRCLE OF SUCCESS

Surrounding yourself with the right people multiplies your potential. Alone, you can go fast. Together, you go *farther, faster, and stronger.*

Here's how to build your Circle of Success:

Role	Purpose	Frequency	Notes
Counselor	Heal the past, rewire your mindset	As needed	Especially when stuck or overwhelmed
Coach	Gain clarity, create strategy, drive execution	Weekly/ Bi-weekly/ Monthly	Hire based on your specific needs
Mentor	Tap into experience and wisdom	Monthly	Can be informal or structured

Accountability Partner	Encourage and challenge you daily	Daily/Weekly	Peer or colleague with shared goals
Accountability Group	Collective energy and momentum	Weekly/ Bi-weekly	Choose wisely—alignment matters
Executive Assistant	Delegate and systematize tasks	Daily/Weekly	Start with automation if needed

DON'T GO IT ALONE

Every visionary needs a village. Every champion needs a coach. Every dreamer needs a team.

So, ask yourself:

- Who's in your corner?
- Who challenges you, supports you, and helps you rise?
- Where are you trying to go it alone when you should be inviting help?

You were never meant to do this solo. So stop white knuckling it. Stop jacking around.

Build your team. Trust the process. Leverage support.

Your next breakthrough could be one conversation away.

SELF-ACCOUNTABILITY TOOLS: LEAD YOURSELF FIRST

While having key accountability relationships is a key to success in achieving your goals, accountability doesn't always require another person. In fact, some of the most powerful forms of accountability begin with *you*. The ability to lead yourself, stay honest about your progress, and reflect consistently is what separates dabblers from disciplined doers.

Here are several self-accountability tools to help you stay aligned, focused, and moving forward, even when no one else is watching.

1. DAILY JOURNALING

A quick five-to-ten-minute habit that helps you:

- Review your Vision-Execution Snapshot.
- Reflect on your mindset and actions.
- Celebrate small wins.
- Identify patterns or recurring challenges.
- Reconnect with your vision and purpose.

Prompt ideas:

- What did I accomplish today that moved me closer to my goals?
- What challenged me, and how did I respond?
- What will I do differently tomorrow?

2. WEEKLY REVIEWS

As outlined earlier in this book, a dedicated time (thirty to sixty minutes) to review your:

- Vision-Execution Snapshot.
- Progress on your top three goals.
- Habits and routines.
- Systems and blockers.
- Energy alignment and time use.

This consistent rhythm builds clarity, momentum, and personal leadership.

3. VISUAL PROGRESS CHARTS

As described earlier in the book, make your habits and milestones visible:

- Use a habit tracker (analog or digital).
- Chart your streaks or percentage of goal completion.
- Create a progress wall or digital dashboard.

Seeing your progress boosts motivation and reinforces follow-through.

4. MONTHLY REPORT TO SELF DOCUMENTS

Once a month, write a personal performance review. Think of it as a leadership meeting with yourself.

Include:

- A review of your Vision-Execution Snapshot.
- Major wins and learnings.
- What worked/what didn't.
- Adjustments for the coming month.
- Recommitment to your values and vision.

You can format this as a letter, a bullet-point report, or a reflective journal entry. The goal is clarity and alignment, not perfection.

Self-accountability is a form of self-respect. When you learn to answer to yourself, you become unstoppable.

ACCOUNTABILITY IS YOUR EDGE

At the end of the day, success doesn't belong to the most talented or the most motivated; it belongs to the most accountable. Whether it's through a coach, mentor, peer group, or your own daily systems, accountability is what turns vision into movement and goals into results. It's what keeps you honest when no one's watching and committed when things get hard. The Personal Success System isn't just about knowing what to do; it's about creating a structure of support that ensures you actually do it. Build it. Join it. Lead it. Your next breakthrough is waiting, and accountability is the key that unlocks it.

SECTION SUMMARY: EXECUTION: SUSTAINING MOMENTUM AND STAYING ACCOUNTABLE

KEY TAKEAWAYS:

- Success arises from consistent, intentional actions aligned with vision and goals.
- Execution converts vision and goals into tangible outcomes, despite resistance or distraction.
- Regular strategic reviews (annual, quarterly, weekly, daily) ensure continued alignment with purpose, values, and vision.
- Effective accountability structures significantly enhance follow-through and goal achievement.

CORE ACTIONS FOR EXECUTION:

1. ANNUAL STRATEGIC REVIEW:

- Schedule one to two days annually (December/January) for deep reflection and strategic planning.
- Revisit mindset, legacy, and vision, and assess progress across the 7 Fs Matrix.
- Review and update your Vision-Execution Snapshot.

- Set clear, inspiring annual goals, breaking them into quarterly milestones and actionable habits.

2. QUARTERLY STRATEGIC REVIEW:

- Allocate at least half a day quarterly for recalibration.
- Review and update your Vision-Execution Snapshot.
- Evaluate alignment with DNA (Purpose + Values), vision, and goals.
- Establish clear quarterly targets, broken down into monthly milestones and defined habits.

3. WEEKLY REVIEW AND PLANNING:

- Set aside thirty to ninety minutes weekly for strategic reflection and realignment.
- Review and update your Vision-Execution Snapshot.
- Identify weekly priorities, obstacles, and wins, and refine execution plans.
- Schedule priorities explicitly using time blocks to ensure progress.

4. DAILY PLANNING:

- Review and update your Vision-Execution Snapshot.
- Conduct daily planning sessions (morning or evening), identifying your top three priorities.
- Use time blocking aligned with daily energy patterns to ensure effective execution.

- Consistently revisit personal vision and purpose for motivation.

ESSENTIAL TOOLS AND STRATEGIES:

- **Habit Stacking:** Anchor new habits to existing ones to automate execution.
- **Time Blocking:** Clearly allocate blocks for deep work, admin tasks, recovery, and strategic goals.
- **Energy-Based Execution:** Align tasks with personal energy rhythms, especially useful for those with dynamic energy patterns like ADHD.

TRACKING SYSTEMS:

- Use habit trackers, goal scorecards, and streak charts to maintain visibility of progress.
- Implement daily and weekly reflection journals for qualitative insights.
- Review and update your Vision-Execution Snapshot.

ACCOUNTABILITY STRUCTURES:

- Engage counselors for resolving past issues and enhancing your mindset.
- Employ coaches for clarity, strategy, accountability, and overcoming execution barriers.
- Seek mentors for experience-based wisdom.
- Establish accountability partnerships/groups for regular check-ins and motivation.

- Delegate tasks to executive assistants or automation tools to free up strategic focus.

SELF-ACCOUNTABILITY TOOLS:

- Daily and weekly reviews of your Vision-Execution Snapshot.
- Maintain daily journaling for reflection and growth.
- Conduct weekly reviews to assess progress and realign goals.
- Utilize visual progress tracking to boost motivation and clarity.
- Generate monthly personal performance reports for deep self-assessment.

EXECUTION FORMULA FOR SUSTAINABLE SUCCESS:

Clarity + Consistency + Regular Review + Robust Accountability = Sustainable Success

CONCLUSION

EXECUTE AND WIN

You've made it to the end of this book, and that is no small feat. By now, you've explored the core principles of success: defining your purpose, crafting your vision, breaking it down into actionable goals, and implementing a system to stay accountable and sustain momentum. Here's the truth: Knowledge alone isn't enough. Success comes from action. The only thing standing between you and your dreams is the decision to start and the discipline to follow through.

As you move forward, remember that the path to success is not a straight line. There will be challenges, setbacks, and moments of doubt. Within those moments lies your greatest opportunity: the chance to persevere, adapt, and grow. The Personal Success System outlined in this book is not just a roadmap; it's your foundation, your guide, and your safety net. It is designed to help you navigate the twists and turns of life while keeping your eyes firmly on your goals.

YOUR CALL TO ACTION

You now hold the tools to:

- Define your purpose and values, the guiding principles that shape your decisions and give your life meaning.
- Craft a vision that inspires you, motivates you, and serves as your compass in moments of uncertainty.
- Break down that vision into actionable steps using The JACKED Framework™
- Build daily, weekly, and quarterly habits that align your actions with your long-term objectives.
- Stay accountable and sustain momentum through tracking, reviews, and the support of coaches or accountability partners.

Tools only work when you use them. This is your call to action. *Execute.* Start today. Take one step, however small, toward the life you've envisioned. Whether it's writing down your goals, setting up a tracking system, or reaching out to an accountability partner, every action matters. The journey of a thousand miles begins with a single step, and that step is yours to take.

WHY YOU WILL WIN

You have everything you need to succeed. The PSS is designed not just to help you set goals but to equip you with the mindset, structure, and tools to achieve them. Remember the stories of individuals who turned obstacles into stepping stones: Michael Jordan, Sara Blakely, Roger Bannister, Oprah Winfrey, and countless others. They were not born with guarantees of success; they earned it through resilience, discipline, and an unwavering belief in their ability to grow and adapt.

You are no different. The same principles that guided their success can guide yours. Believe that you can overcome challenges, embrace failure as a teacher, and stay committed to your vision. Success is not reserved for the few; it's available to anyone willing to do the work. And you are capable of doing the work.

A FINAL WORD OF ENCOURAGEMENT

You are the architect of your life. Every decision you make, every habit you build, and every goal you pursue shapes the legacy you leave behind. This is your time to take control, to stop settling for less, and to start building the life you deserve.

As you move forward, keep these words in mind.

- Your results won't exceed the consistency of your daily structure.
- "Success isn't always about greatness. It's about consistency. Consistent hard work leads to success. Greatness will come." —Dwayne Johnson
- "The journey of a thousand miles begins with a single step." —Lao Tzu

The systems and strategies you've learned in this book are your foundation. Build on them. Refine them. Trust in the process. Most importantly, trust in yourself. You have the potential to achieve extraordinary things. Now it's time to turn that potential into reality.

Go out there and execute. Go out there and win. Your future self is waiting.

Are you ready to commit to your future success? A commitment to your PSS is required to succeed. If you fail to commit, you will fail to succeed.

QUIT JACKING AROUND PERSONAL SUCCESS SYSTEM COMMITMENT

Read this aloud. Feel its weight. Then, put your name to it and make it real.

I, _____,
recognizing that time is my most precious, non-renewable asset, hereby commit to **Quit Jacking Around** and to build the Personal Success System outlined in this book.

1. **Mindset**   I will cultivate a growth-and-abundance outlook, reject limiting beliefs, and replace excuses with action.
2. **DNA (Purpose + Values)**   I will discover, name, and align my deepest *why*, letting my values steer every decision.
3. **Vision**   I will craft a vivid picture of the future I am called to create and review it regularly.
4. **Goals**   I will translate that vision into written, measurable goals, broken into quarterly and daily targets.

5. **Execution and Accountability**   I will track my progress, celebrate small wins, course-correct quickly, and seek trusted accountability partners.
6. **Service and Integrity**   I will use the momentum I gain to serve others, lead with integrity, and multiply positive impact.

I understand that success is not an event but a practice—a daily choice to take the next right step. By signing below, I pledge to act on the principles in these pages, to measure my growth, and to persevere when motivation fades.

Should I falter, I will return to this commitment, remember my purpose, and begin again—because my future, my family, and my legacy are worth the effort.

Signature: _____   **Date:** _____

(Optional) **Accountability Partner / Witness:** _____

Keep a copy of this page where you'll see it every day—on your desk, mirror, or inside the front cover of this book. Read it whenever you need a shot of resolve. Your future self will thank you.

ENDNOTES

1. Clear, James. *Atomic Habits: An Easy & Proven Way to Build Good Habits & Break Bad Ones.* New York: Avery, 2018.
2. Rosenfield, Leah. "2024 Statistics on New Year's Resolutions." 2024 Statistics on New Year's Resolutions. December 27, 2023. https://sesamecare.com/blog/new-years-resolution-survey.
3. "19 Surprising New Year's Resolution Statistics (2024 Updated)." Insideout Mastery. September 2, 2024. https://insideoutmastery.com/new-years-resolution-statistics/.
4. "New Year's Resolution Statistics (2023 Updated)." Discover Happy Habits. June 1, 2024. https://discoverhappyhabits.com/new-years-resolution-statistics/.
5. Maatta, Petri. "New Years Resolutions Statistics (2023 - 2024)." DreamMaker. July 3, 2024. https://dreammakerr.com/new-years-resolutions-statistics/.
6. "19 Surprising New Year's Resolution Statistics (2024 Updated)."
7. Batts, Richard. "Why Most New Year's Resolutions Fail: Lead Read Today." Fisher College of Business. February 2, 2023. https://fisher.osu.edu/blogs/leadreadtoday/why-most-new-years-resolutions-fail.
8. "19 Surprising New Year's Resolution Statistics (2024 Updated)."
9. "19 Surprising New Year's Resolution Statistics (2024 Updated)."
10. Batts.

11 Maatta.

12 "19 Surprising New Year's Resolution Statistics (2024 Updated)."

13 "19 Surprising New Year's Resolution Statistics (2024 Updated)."

14 Nina. "How Many People Reach Their Goals? Goal Statistics 2024." Goals Calling. January 28, 2024. https://goalscalling.com/goal-statistics/.

15 Wilczek, Frank. "Einstein's Parable of Quantum Insanity." *Scientific American*. February 20, 2024. https://www.scientificamerican.com/article/einstein-s-parable-of-quantum-insanity/.

16 Wilson, Rachel. *Uyghur Heritage Language Teacher Handbook*. Texas Scholar Works. University of Texas at Austin. June 21, 2024. https://doi.org/10.26153/tsw/52421.

17 Berler, Richard. "Michael Jordan: A Profile in Failure." *Newsweek*. October 24, 2015. Accessed August 5, 2025. https://www.newsweek.com/missing-cut-382954.

18 Britannica Editors. "Michael Jordan." *Encyclopedia Britannica*. December 9, 2025. https://www.britannica.com/biography/Michael-Jordan.

19 Nike. *Failure* commercial, narrated by Michael Jordan. 1997. https://www.youtube.com/watch?v=45mMioJ5szc.

20 Haverstock, Eliza. "Sara Blakely Is a Billionaire (Again) After Selling a Majority of Spanx to Blackstone." *Forbes*. October 20, 2021. https://www.google.com/url?q=https://www.forbes.com/sites/elizahaverstock/2021/10/20/sara-blakely-is-a-billionaire-again-after-selling-a-majority-of-spanx-to-blackstone/&sa=D&source=docs&ust=1764784629815844&usg=AOvVaw1PW2zvHSf83gNdOm5doFjv.

21 "The Spanx Startup Story." *Fundable*. https://www.fundable.com/learn/startup-stories/spanx.

22 "The Sara Blakely Foundation," The Sara Blakely Foundation, accessed July 8, 2025, https://www.redbackpackfoundation.org/.

23 Nike, *Failure* commercial.

24 Hill, Napoleon. *Think and Grow Rich*. Meriden, CT: The Ralston Society, 1937.

25 Gates, Bill. "Teachers Need Real Feedback." filmed May 2013, TED video, 10:22, https://www.ted.com/talks/bill_gates_teachers_need_real_feedback.

26 Emmons, Robert A. *Thanks! How the New Science of Gratitude Can Make You Happier*. Boston: Houghton Mifflin Harcourt, 2007.

27 Bartoli, Nicola and Simone Benedetto. "Driven by Notifications–Exploring the Effects of Badge Notifications on User Experience." *PLOS ONE* 17, no. 6 (2022): e0270888.

28 Staff. "The Dunning-Kruger Effect." *Psychology Today*. Accessed December 3, 2025. *https://www.psychologytoday.com/us/basics/dunning-kruger-effect#:~:text=The%20Dunning%2DKruger%20effect%20is%20a%20cognitive%20bias,them%20from%20accurately%20assessing%20their%20own%20skills.*

29 Bannister, Roger. *The Four-Minute Mile*. Guilford, CT: Lyons Press, 2004; Bascomb, Neal. *The Perfect Mile: Three Athletes, One Goal, and Less Than Four Minutes to Achieve It*. Boston: Houghton Mifflin Harcourt, 2004; Dweck, Carol S. *Mindset: The New Psychology of Success*. New York: Random House, 2006.

30 Klein, Christopher. "The first 4-minute mile, 60 years ago." History.com. Retrieved October 25, 2025, from https://www.history.com/articles/the-first-4-minute-mile-60-years-ago.

31 Klein.

32 Bannister.

33 Klein.

34 Klein.

35 Dyer, F. L., and T. C. Martin. *Edison: His Life and Inventions.* 2 vols. New York: Harper & Brothers, 1910.

36 Oxford University Press. Entry "Thomas Alva Edison, 1847–1931." Oxford Reference. Accessed December 3, 2025. https://www.oxfordreference.com/display/10.1093/oi/authority.20110803095742410?rskey=faPkoY&result=1

37 Maxwell, John C. *Failing Forward: Turning Mistakes into Stepping Stones for Success.* Nashville: Thomas Nelson, 2007.

38 BBC News. "JK Rowling: The story of her early struggles and how she became a success." July 31, 2017. Retrieved November 7, 2025. https://www.bbc.com/news/uk-40770771.

39 "J. K. Rowling." Biography.com. Accessed November 7, 2025. https://www.biography.com/authors-writers/jk-rowling.

40 BBC News.

41 BBC News.

42 Biography.com.

43 BBC News.

44 Biography.com.

45 Biography.com.

46 BBC News.

47 Hill, Patrick L., Nicholas A. Turiano, Alan Spiro III, and Daniel K. Mroczek, "Purpose in Life as a Predictor of Mortality across Adulthood." *Psychosomatic Medicine* 78, no. 6 (2016): 612–19. https://doi.org/10.1097/PSY.0000000000000346.

48 Ericsson, K. Anders, Ralf T. Krampe, and Clemens Tesch-Römer. "The Role of Deliberate Practice in the Acquisition of Expert Performance." *Psychological Review* 100, no. 3 (1993): 363–406. https://doi.org/10.1037/0033-295X.100.3.363.

49 Steger, Michael F. "Meaning in Life." In *The Encyclopedia of Positive Psychology*, edited by Shane J. Lopez, 605-10. Vol. 2. Chichester, UK: Wiley-Blackwell, 2009.

50 Bandura, Albert. *Self-Efficacy: The Exercise of Control.* New York: W. H. Freeman, 1997.

51 Deci, Edward L., and Richard M. Ryan, "The 'What' and 'Why' of Goal Pursuits: Human Needs and the Self-Determination of Behavior." *Psychological Inquiry* 11, no. 4 (2000): 227–68. https://doi.org/10.1207/S15327965PLI1104_01.

52 Sheldon, Kennon M., and Andrew J. Elliot, "Goal Striving, Need Satisfaction, and Longitudinal Well-Being: The Self-Concordance Model," *Journal of Personality and Social Psychology* 76, no. 3 (1999): 482–97.

53 Sheldon, Kennon M., and Laurie Houser-Marko, "Self-Concordance, Goal Attainment, and the Pursuit of Happiness: Can There Be an Upward Spiral?" *Journal of Personality and Social Psychology,* 80, no. 1 (2001): 152–65. https://pubmed.ncbi.nlm.nih.gov/11195887/.

54 Deci, Edward L., and Richard M. Ryan. "The 'What' and 'Why' of Goal Pursuits: Human Needs and the Self-Determination of Behavior." *Psychological Inquiry* 11, no. 4 (2000): 227–68.

55 Koestner, Roy, Nathalie Lekes, Tara A. Powers, and Emilie Chicoine. "Attaining Personal Goals: Self-Concordance Plus Implementation Intentions Equals Success." *Journal of Personality and Social Psychology* 83, no. 1 (2002): 231–44.

56 Milyavskaya, Mariya et al. "Self-Determined Motivation, Goals, and Goal Progress." *Journal of Personality* 83, no. 3 (2015): 256–66.

57 Hill, Patrick L., Alexander L. Burrow, and Kendall C. Bronk. "Persevering with Positivity and Purpose: An Examination of Purpose Commitment and Positive Affect as Predictors of Grit." *Journal of Happiness Studies* 17, no. 1 (2016): 257–69.

58 Deci and Ryan, "The 'What' and 'Why' of Goal Pursuits."

59 Sheldon and Houser-Marko, "Self-Concordance, Goal Attainment, and the Pursuit of Happiness."

60. Koestner et al., "Attaining Personal Goals."
61. Schippers, Michaéla C., and Nicolai Ziegler. "Life Crafting as a Way to Find Purpose and Meaning in Life." *Frontiers in Psychology* 10 (2019): 2778. https://doi.org/10.3389/fpsyg.2019.02778.
62. Gallup. *State of the Global Workplace*. Washington, DC: Gallup Press, 2017.
63. Ayse Alimujiang et al. "Association between Life Purpose and Mortality among US Adults Older than 50 Years." *JAMA Network Open* 2, no. 5 (2019): e194270. https://doi.org/10.1001/jamanetworkopen.2019.4270.
64. Burrow, Alexander L., and Patrick L. Hill. "Purpose as a Form of Identity Capital for Positive Youth Adjustment." *Developmental Psychology* 47, no. 4 (2011): 1196–1202.
65. Schippers and Ziegler, "Life Crafting as a Way to Find Purpose and Meaning in Life."
66. Ryff, Carol D., and Burton Singer. "The Contours of Positive Human Health." *Psychological Inquiry*, 9, no. 1 (1998): 1–28.
67. Ugwueke. "How Olympic Athletes Use Visualization Techniques to Win Gold." GlobalSports360. https://globalsports360.com/2025/07/28/how-olympic-athletes-use-visualization-techniques-to-win-gold/; MindSense Academy. "The Power of Visualization: How Michael Phelps Used Mental Imagery to Win Gold." MindSense Academy. February 3, 2025. https://mindsense.academy/the-power-of-visualization-how-michael-phelps-used-mental-imagery-to-win-gold/.
68. Faller, Mary Beth. "Bob Bowman Uses Michael Phelps to Explain How to Achieve Excellence." ASU Now. January 30, 2017. https://news.asu.edu/20170130-sun-devil-life-bob-bowman-uses-michael-phelps-explain-how-achieve-excellence#:~:text=The%20high%2Dperformance%20phase%20is,your%20GPS%2C%E2%80%9D%20he%20said.
69. Ugwueke; MindSense Academy.

70 Faller.

71 Ugwueke; MindSense Academy.

72 Meier, J. D. "How Michael Phelps Used Visualization to Break World Records." Sources of Insight. Accessed December 4, 2025. https://sourcesofinsight.com/how-michael-phelps-used-visualization/.

73 Matthews, Gail. "The Impact of Commitment, Accountability, and Written Goals on Goal Achievement." *Psychology Faculty Presentations*, no. 3 (2007). Dominican University of California. https://scholar.dominican.edu/psychology-faculty-conference-presentations/3.

74 Locke, Edwin A. and Gary P. Latham. *A Theory of Goal Setting and Task Performance.* Englewood Cliffs, NJ: Prentice Hall, 1990.

75 Fox, Kieran C. R. et al. "Functional Neuroanatomy of Meditation: A Review and Meta-Analysis of 78 Functional Neuroimaging Investigations." *bioRxiv.* March 21, 2016. https://doi.org/10.1101/045269.

76 Dae Seok Chai, Seog Joo Hwang, and Baek-Kyoo Joo, "Transformational Leadership and Organizational Commitment in Teams: The Mediating Roles of Shared Vision and Team-Goal Commitment," *Performance Improvement Quarterly* 30, no. 2 (July 2017): 137–58, https://doi.org/10.1002/piq.21244.

77 Positive Psychology Center. "Life Satisfaction and Vision Correlation." University of Pennsylvania. Accessed July 19, 2025. https://ppc.sas.upenn.edu/life-satisfaction-and-vision-correlation.

78 GoalsCalling. "SMART Goals and Success Rate Study." GoalsCalling.com. Accessed July 19, 2025. https://www.goalscalling.com/smart-goals-and-success-rte-study.

79 Collins, Jim C., and Jerry I. Porras. *Built to Last: Successful Habits of Visionary Companies.* New York: HarperBusiness, 1994.

80. Locke, E. A., and G. P. Latham. "Building a practically useful theory of goal setting and task motivation: A 35-year odyssey." *American Psychologist*, 57, no. 9 (2002), 705–717. https://doi.org/10.1037/0003-066X.57.9.705; Höpfner, J., and Keith, N. "High goals can undermine motivation: Goal difficulty, performance, and self-regulation outcomes." *Frontiers in Psychology* 45, no. 3, (2021): 259–273. doi: 10.3389/fpsyg.2021.704790.

81. Ravishankar, Rakshitha Arni, and Kelsey Alpaio. "5 Ways to Set More Achievable Goals." August 30, 2022. https://hbr.org/2022/08/5-ways-to-set-more-achievable-goals.

82. White Paper. "The Executive Guide to Goal Setting: Common Pitfalls, Popular Approaches and Best Practices from Goal Setting Executives." AchieveIt. Accessed December 12, 2025. https://www.achieveit.com/confirmation/guide-executive-guide-strategic-goal-setting/.

83. Höpfner, J., and N. Keith.

84. Cascio, Christopher N., Matthew B. O'Donnell, Francis J. Tinney, Matthew D. Lieberman, Shelley E. Taylor, Victor J. Strecher, and Emily B. Falk. "Self-Affirmation Activates Brain Systems Associated with Self-Related Processing and Reward and Is Reinforced by Future Orientation." *Social Cognitive and Affective Neuroscience* 11, no. 4 (2016): 621–29. https://doi.org/10.1093/scan/nsv136.

85. Cascio et al., "Self-Affirmation Activates Brain Systems."

86. Conlon, Ciara. "Efficiency through Affirmations: A Science-Based Approach." *Ciara Mindset*. March 10, 2024. https://ciaraconlon.com/2024/efficiency-through-affirmations-a-science-based-approach/.

87. Brown, C. "The Power of Positive Affirmations." *Comprehensive Healthcare*. January 22, 2024. https://comphc.org/the-power-of-positive-affirmations/.

88. Koosis, Lisa A. "The Science of Affirmations: The Brain's Response to Positive Thinking." MentalHealth.com. https://www.mentalhealth.com/tools/science-of-affirmations.

89 Cascio et al., "Self-Affirmation Activates Brain Systems."

90 Moore, Catherine. "Positive Daily Affirmations: Is There Science Behind It?" PositivePsychology.com. March 4, 2019. https://positivepsychology.com/daily-affirmations/.

91 Gilbert, Kylie. "Affirmations Really Work: Here's How to Use Them to Reach Your Personal Goals." Peloton Blog. June 19, 2024. https://www.onepeloton.com/blog/what-are-affirmations/.

92 Conlon.

93 *Peloton Blog.*

94 *Peloton Blog.*

95 Conlon.

96 Brown.

97 Brown.

98 Duhigg, Charles. *The Power of Habit: Why We Do What We Do in Life and Business.* New York: Random House, 2023.

99 Duhigg.

100 Wikipedia. "Wilma Rudolph." Accessed December 8, 2025. https://en.wikipedia.org/wiki/Wilma_Rudolph.

101 Anderson, Erica. "Wilma Rudolph (1940–1994)." BlackPast.org. March 14, 2007. https://www.blackpast.org/african-american-history/rudolph-wilma-1940-1994/.

102 Britannica Editors. "Wilma Rudolph." *Encyclopedia Britannica*, November 8, 2025. https://www.britannica.com/biography/Wilma-Rudolph.

103 Anderson.

104 Anderson.

105 Yang, Avery. "Black History Month: Remembering Wilma Rudolph's Unlikely Journey to Olympic Gold." *Sports Illustrated.* February 6, 2020. https://www.si.com/olympics/2020/02/06/black-history-month-wilma-rudolph-legacy.

106 Anderson.

107 Anderson.

108 Anderson.

109 Wikipedia, "Wilma Rudolph."

110 Wikipedia, "Wilma Rudolph."

111 Wikipedia, "Wilma Rudolph."

112 Encyclopædia Britannica, "Wilma Rudolph."

113 Wikipedia, "Wilma Rudolph."

114 Yang.

115 Anderson.

116 Yang.

117 Lake, T., and J. Hibler. "Bethany Hamilton." Encyclopedia Britannica, October 11, 2025. https://www.britannica.com/biography/Bethany-Hamilton.

118 Inspire & Rise. "Bethany Hamilton: Surviving a Shark Attack," Inspire & Rise. Accessed December 8, 2025. https://www.inspireandrise.com/bethany-hamilton-surviving-a-shark-attack/.

119 Lake, T., and J. Hibler.

120 Lake, T., and J. Hibler.

121 Medrano, Kastalia. "Surfer Bethany Hamilton Describes How Shark Attack Shaped Her Faith." *Time.* November 2, 2016. https://time.com/bethany-hamilton-shark-attack-faith.

122 "Welcome to Innovation." Bethany Hamilton Official Website. Accessed December 12, 2025. https://bethanyhamilton.com/blog/welcome-to-innovation

123 "Bethany's Story." Bethany Hamilton Official Website. Accessed August 9, 2025. https://www.bethanyhamilton.com/pages/bethanys-story.

124 Kazimierska, Marika. "Bethany Hamilton's Horrific Accident and Life After." Nicki Swift. January 25, 2023, https://www.nickiswift.com/1178810/bethany-hamiltons-horrific-accident-and-life-after/.

125 "Bethany's Story."

126 "Bethany's Story."
127 Ugwueke. "Bethany Hamilton: The Unstoppable Soul Surfer Who Redefined Resilience in Sports." GlobalSports360. April 23, 2025. https://globalsports360.com/2025/04/23/bethany-hamilton-the-unstoppable-soul-surfer-who-redefined-resilience-in-sports/.
128 "Bethany's Story."
129 Rohn, *The Five Major Pieces to the Life Puzzle*.
130 Wissman, Barrett. "An Accountability Partner Makes You Vastly More Likely to Succeed." *Entrepreneur*. March 20, 2018. https://www.entrepreneur.com/leadership/an-accountability-partner-makes-you-vastly-more-likely-to/310062.

ACKNOWLEDGMENTS

First and foremost, I give thanks to God for uniquely creating and equipping me—for giving me the strengths, abilities, and life experiences that made it possible to write this book. Every insight, opportunity, and step along the way has been guided by His hand, and I am grateful for His constant presence and provision.

I would also like to thank the many leaders, writers, podcasters, and friends whose teachings and insights have shaped my thinking and fueled my growth. Your wisdom and example have been instrumental in helping me develop both the content and the heart behind this book and the system it presents.

My gratitude also goes to my publisher and the entire team at Igniting Souls. Thank you for believing in this project, refining its message, and guiding it from concept to completion. Your expertise, dedication, and passion for bringing ideas to life made it possible for this book to reach the hands and hearts of readers.

This work would not have been possible without my incredible teams at Aeris Insurance Solutions and Aereach Strategic Partners. In particular, I want to recognize my Strategic Partner, Jolina; our IT and Operations Lead, Nick; and our Marketing Officer, Keen. Your dedication, creativity, and hard work were essential in bringing this vision to life, and I am truly thankful for each of you.

Finally, to my family—Morgan, Trip, Mimi, Eli, and Ben—thank you for your constant support, encouragement, and love. You are my greatest blessing and my greatest motivation.

ABOUT THE AUTHOR

Tim Bonnell Jr. is the Founder, President, and CEO of Aeris Insurance Solutions, a trusted advisor in aviation insurance and risk management solutions. He is the author of three industry-focused books: *Airport and Aviation Business Insurance Fundamentals: A Concise Guide for Airports and Aviation Businesses*, *Aircraft Insurance Fundamentals: A Concise Guide for Aircraft Owners and Operators – Revised and Expanded 2nd Edition*, and *Aerial Application Insurance Fundamentals: A Concise Guide for Aerial Application Operations*. Tim also hosts the Aviation Insurance Podcast, a go-to resource for professionals seeking insights into the complexities of aviation insurance.

As a third-generation pilot and second-generation aviation insurance broker, Tim was raised in the aviation insurance industry, learning it from the ground up. He is a private and instrument-rated pilot and holds the Certified Aviation Insurance Professional (CAIP) and Certified Insurance Counselor (CIC) designations. A proud alumnus of Kansas State University, Tim's dedication to excellence earned him induction into the inaugural class of the Aviation Insurance Association's (AIA) Eagle Society in 2014.

Tim has served on the boards of directors of the AIA, the Kansas Agricultural Aviation Association, the National Agricultural Aviation Association, and the Wichita Aero Club, among others. He is the Past Chair of the AIA's Education Committee and continues to lead as one of their primary instructors, advancing the next generation of aviation insurance professionals. He's also a CBMC-certified Leadership Coach Trainer.

In addition to his work with Aeris Insurance Solutions, Tim Bonnell Jr. is the visionary CEO of Aereach Strategic Partners, which provides transformative remote back-office staffing and solutions to entrepreneurial businesses. At Aereach, the mission goes beyond staffing—it's about creating life-changing careers for remote professionals while driving exceptional results for clients.

Born out of the need to address operational challenges, such as finding and retaining quality talent, Aereach simplifies the complexity of building and managing global remote teams. The company takes an end-to-end approach, offering not just candidates but fully integrated solutions that include recruiting, onboarding, training, and ongoing support. This process ensures long-term success for both clients and team members, fostering a community of trust, growth, and excellence.

Tim's career reflects a lifelong commitment to innovation, leadership, and empowering others—whether in aviation insurance or by transforming the way businesses achieve operational excellence worldwide. His passion for educating and inspiring others is evident in his work as an author, speaker, and mentor, making him a respected thought leader in both the aviation and business communities. He has developed the Personal Success System by starting numerous profit and non-profit organizations. Tim's passion for helping others reach their goals is why this book was written.

Transform your future.

Quit Jacking Around™
is more than a book,
it's your entry point into the
Personal Success System™
(PSS), built to help you align
your values, vision, and
daily actions.

PSS Tools

yourpss.com

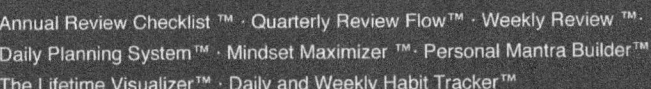

Annual Review Checklist ™ · Quarterly Review Flow™ · Weekly Review ™·
Daily Planning System™ · Mindset Maximizer ™· Personal Mantra Builder™
The Lifetime Visualizer™ · Daily and Weekly Habit Tracker™

Your Growth Starts with the Right Team.

At **Aereach Strategic Partners**™, we connect you with elite remote professionals who allow you to focus on what matters most. From executive assistants to marketing experts, we deliver tailored support designed to integrate seamlessly into your operations and help you build the team that brings your vision to life.

Executive Assistants | Bookkeeping & Accounting
Marketing & Content Creation | Customer Service &
Project Coordination | I.T. & Security Support |
HR & Recruitment and more!

aereachpartners.com

www.ingramcontent.com/pod-product-compliance
Lightning Source LLC
Chambersburg PA
CBHW070042120526
44589CB00035B/2081